Praise for DO LIFE DIFFERENTLY

"Jeff Reeter's book, DO LIFE DIFFERENTLY, is about purpose, discipline, determination, and the importance of always being your best for your God, family, career, and the generations that follow. I especially recommend the book to young professionals."

—**ARCHIE DUNHAM**, chairman, president, and CEO, Conoco; chairman, ConocoPhillips; and chairman, Chesapeake Energy (retired)

"My friend Jeff Reeter has written an extraordinary book. The life systems contained in DO LIFE DIFFERENTLY have been used by Jeff and others who have been impacted by his life and leadership to enhance the probability of broader success, greater adventure, and outcomes beyond the ordinary. I sincerely appreciate that Jeff measures 'extraordinary' in a multidimensional way to include faith, family, fitness, community leadership, friendship, development, and so much more. This is a unique kind of book on how to live the best life you possibly can. It requires you to be proactive in leading yourself—by design—and not to simply allow life to happen to you—by default. This book will be well worth your read."

—**STEVE GREEN**, president, Hobby Lobby Stores, Inc., and chairman of the board, Museum of the Bible

"One of the great truths we need to accept is that God is big enough to create a unique plan for each of us. None of us need nor should want to merely replicate someone else's life. It would be a waste of the one-of-a-kind life the Creator intends for each of us. Jeff Reeter makes that truth practical in his dynamic book DO LIFE DIFFERENTLY. From a super successful business career,

Jeff approaches life with passion, purpose, and a plan. His message will stick to your ribs—and your heart—and you'll probably decide to 'do life differently.'"

—**MIKE HUCKABEE**, governor of Arkansas, 1996–2007

"In this book, Jeff Reeter does an amazing job of sharing life experiences and turns them into priceless principles on how to purposefully live life differently. DO LIFE DIFFERENTLY is a must-read for every leader."

—**MAC McQUISTON**, founder, CEO Forum

"Jeff Reeter has been a leader all his life. As a member of our 1980 to 1984 Baylor football team, Jeff was a letterman but never a starter, demonstrating a keen sense of leadership and coachability as an athlete. He studied the game and knew what it was about inside and out. He was personable and executed his part of the game for the success of the team. I know that Jeff applied those same principles beyond football as a husband, father, businessman, and adventurer. When you read DO LIFE DIFFERENTLY you will discover how true prosperity and legacy begin when you live life by design and not default. This is a great book to help anyone learn how to live their best life."

—**GRANT TEAFF**, former head football coach, Baylor University, and former executive director, American Football Coaches Association

"I enjoyed reading and learning from DO LIFE DIFFERENTLY. As someone who has known Jeff for years, it is clear he is extraordinarily accomplished, and this book is a great how-to guide for anyone wanting to live their best life...and don't we all?"

—**DAVID WEEKLEY**, chairman, David Weekley Homes

"I know Jeff Reeter well as a past employee and very close friend. He's not superman (because Superman had a kryptonite issue!). He IS one of the most 'super' individuals on the planet because he is one of the very few national leaders who lives life in remarkable ways as a dad, a husband, a business leader, a developer of others, a church leader, and a man who humbles himself daily and intentionally with his Creator and Savior. One conversation with Jeff is often life changing. Imagine what a continual conversation can do as you meld your heart with his through your study of this remarkable book."

—**DR. JOE WHITE**, president, Kanakuk Ministries

"Jeff Reeter's DO LIFE DIFFERENTLY artfully articulates Jeff's strategy for a leadership style that is purposeful, planned, disciplined, and driven by an unswerving commitment to excellence. Not only have I described the strategy, I have described the author. Jeff is one of the few people who live out what they profess. Woven throughout the pages of the book is the not-so-secret ingredient to Reeter's blueprint for success: Jesus. Jeff follows a Leader who also calls us to do life differently. This is a refreshing read that mixes the practical with the sacred, and gives the reader a playbook for maximizing opportunities, both God-given and earned.

—**DR. EDWIN YOUNG**, pastor, Second Baptist Church, Houston

"In his inspirational guide on how to pursue a life of purpose and significance, Jeff Reeter speaks from his wildly successful experience in the financial services world, as well as his having boldly scaled our country's highest mountain peaks. Jeff writes with an absorbing combination of passion and humility. DO LIFE DIFFERENTLY provides real-life examples of reaching the summit.

This must-read book brilliantly describes how to find and achieve your dream."

—**KEN STARR**, attorney and *New York Times* bestselling author

"DO LIFE DIFFERENTLY is a powerful new look at leadership. Jeff Reeter shares his experience, wisdom, and integrity in a fascinating and quick read. There are lessons that will make all of us better in this book. I strongly recommend that people searching for their path forward read this book. It will inspire and challenge you."

—**BILL SIMON**, president and CEO, Walmart, US (retired)

"Thomas Sowell once said that most people get through life giving 90 percent when 10 percent more would make them a rock star. A little well-placed effort is the difference between being *ordinary* and *extraordinary*. In Jeff Reeter's book, you will learn step-by-step how you can lead yourself with the skills God gave you to reach for the stars and enjoy a purposeful and fulfilling and extraordinary life."

—**KEN ELDRED**, author, *The Integrated Life* and *God Is at Work*, Silicon Valley entrepreneur, and successful venture investor

"In the midst of everything happening with COVID, the economy, political divisiveness, and racial injustice debates, it brings you back home to what's really important in life. In our fast-moving and stress-filled lives, it is more important than ever to understand that we must each be able to lead ourselves and to know what to do to direct our lives with purpose. In DO LIFE DIFFERENTLY, Jeff Reeter provides you with the tools and strategies you will need for getting a handle on life. It all starts with you, what you are, what your values are, and what are your core competencies. I will make sure that all of my adult children read this book."

—**MIKE SINGLETARY**, NFL Hall of Fame linebacker, Chicago Bears

"The underlying message of DO LIFE DIFFERENTLY—to live by design rather than default—is a crucial message for our world to hear. Jeff describes in great detail how to live by design and make the most of our time on earth. This book is timely, heart-warming, and inspiring!"

—**LINDA A. LIVINGSTONE**, PhD, president, Baylor University

"Jeff has a remarkable track record of developing people AND developing leaders. He has done an amazing job using an approach all his own. DO LIFE DIFFERENTLY lays out Jeff's principles in a readable way that should benefit anyone who takes advantage of his knowledge. In reading this it's clear why Jeff has been so successful."

—**JOHN SCHILFSKE**, chairman and CEO, Northwestern Mutual

DO LIFE DIFFERENTLY

A STRATEGIC PATH TOWARD EXTRAORDINARY

JEFF D. REETER

WITH KRIS BEARSS

WORTHY®

New York • Nashville

Worthy
Hachette Book Group
1290 Avenue of the Americas, New York, NY 10104
worthypublishing.com
twitter.com/worthypub

First Edition: November 2020

Worthy is a division of Hachette Book Group, Inc. The Worthy name and logo are trademarks of Hachette Book Group, Inc.

The publisher is not responsible for websites (or their content) that are not owned by the publisher.

The Hachette Speakers Bureau provides a wide range of authors for speaking events. To find out more, go to www.hachettespeakersbureau.com or call (866) 376-6591.

Library of Congress Cataloging-in-Publication Data
Names: Reeter, Jeff D., author. | Bearss, Kris, author.
Title: Do life differently : a strategic path toward extraordinary / Jeff D. Reeter, with Kris Bearss.
Description: First Edition. | New York : Worthy, 2020. | Includes bibliographical references. |
Summary: "With this essential guide from a successful businessman, start living with intention and abundance by mapping out your B.E.S.T. life of Balance, Excellence, Service, and Truth. While there are numerous podcasts and TED talks that speak about leading others and developing leaders, there are far fewer on the importance of leading yourself. Jeff Reeter will show you how to develop a customized game plan to reach your individual goals and dreams. Do Life Differently is a different kind of book on how to live the best life you possibly can. When you lead yourself well, you create a legacy through which others inherit your character, wisdom, and values that help them on their way"—Provided by publisher.
Identifiers: LCCN 2020022709 | ISBN 9781546036920 (Hardcover) | ISBN 9781546036937 (eBook)
Subjects: LCSH: Self-actualization (Psychology) | Motivation (Psychology) | Personal coaching. | Success.
Classification: LCC BF637.S4 R4474 2020 | DDC 158—dc23
LC record available at https://lccn.loc.gov/2020022709

ISBNs: 978-1-5460-3692-0 (hardcover), 978-1-5460-3691-3 (ebook)

Printed in the United States of America

LSC-C

1 2020

To Team Reeter:
What an extraordinary journey of life we are on.
I'm so proud of each of our Reeter boys:
Chad, Ryan, and Cody.
I'm so grateful to Cindy, my bride, best friend,
and traveling companion.
Ride forth victoriously,
Jeff

What is the use of living, if it be not to strive for noble causes and to make this muddled world a better place for those who will live in it after we are gone?…I avow my faith that we are marching toward better days…We are going on swinging bravely forward along the grand high road and already behind the distant mountains is the promise of the sun.

—Winston Churchill

CONTENTS

FOREWORD

Benjamin S. Carson Sr., MD

Professor Emeritus of Neurosurgery, Oncology, Plastic Surgery,
and Pediatrics, Johns Hopkins Medicine

In this important book, my friend Jeff Reeter tackles a topic that is
near and dear to me, especially given my life's experiences. Whether
you are just getting started in life or well along the way, you need to
know what you can do to invest well in making certain that you are
living to meaningfully benefit others while giving yourself the satisfaction of creating a life of significance.

Ordinary people can accomplish extraordinary things. The life
systems in this book have been found tried and true for enhancing
the probability of broader success, greater adventure, and outcomes

beyond the ordinary. Readers will find that they can intentionally map out their lives toward an extraordinary pursuit of abundance and adventure through leading themselves, instead of following someone else's ideas or plans for them. So many people in our world today, young and old, are lost without direction, and often they are not even aware of it.

I was fortunate to become aware at a young age that I was lost. I started on my journey of intentionality at age fourteen. My life took on a very different trajectory after I decided that I was the one responsible for taking control of my anger as well as the circumstances in which I found myself on a daily basis. My life has been extremely different than it could have been when, at such an early age, I began to understand the importance of leading myself.

In *Do Life Differently*, Jeff shows the reader that the person who has the most to do with the outcome of your life is YOU. You determine your goals and you determine how much energy you will devote to accomplishing them. That goes for relationships as well. This book will help you take control of your life and move forward with intentional ownership of your future.

TAKING THE LEAD

Jeff Turner

Business executive at Willis Towers Watson

It was one of those rare moments in life, when your past, present, and future all connect in such a seamless way that it can't be coincidental.

The young job candidate sitting at the conference table in our corporate office in Houston reminded me of *me*, fresh out of college, if you flashed back twenty-some years! Different company, different era, *different haircut* for sure. But Chad was just as intent on being selective about his first job out of Baylor University as I had been.

I could tell from his thoughtful interview answers that his selectivity wasn't due to a sense of entitlement or ego, but because he apparently understood something that not all twenty-one-year-olds know: If he chose well in this first job, the payoffs in his future would be far greater than any paycheck. If the work aligned with both his personal and professional passions and goals, he would be stepping out into a life for himself, not just a career.

It would be a critical decision. He clearly intended to choose wisely.

After seeing so much of myself in this young man, I was even more grateful that I had Jeff Reeter around to help when I was navigating those kinds of decisions after college and beyond.

Jeff and I were introduced by mutual family friends while I was exploring job options during *my* senior year at Baylor. At that time, Jeff was a financial representative at Northwestern Mutual's Dallas office, and he wanted me to join his record-setting sales team. As a global leader in the financial-services industries, Northwestern certainly had a lot to offer someone like me. So did Jeff. I intuitively sensed he could teach me a lot. For several reasons, however, I didn't feel the company was the best fit for me. So, while I respectfully declined Jeff's job offer, I did take the opportunity to ask, "But can we have breakfast once a month?"

It was a deciding moment in my life. Not only because I was turning down a remarkable opportunity to set my own course, but because I was connecting with someone who would prove to be a primary influence for years to come.

I joined an accounting firm in Dallas instead. Meanwhile, Jeff and I started meeting monthly. And from those conversations, I picked up that two of Jeff Reeter's most-used words are *plan* and *engage*. He doesn't simply mean, "Engage *a* plan." He means, "Engage *your* plan and the people who will be part of it." Determine *your* brand of excellence, and then go after it.

This was my first introduction to "doing life differently" and *leading myself*—Jeff's focus for living by design, not by default. And I needed this concept, because my motto at the beginning of my career was, "Be awesome at work, and everything else will just fall into place." I particularly thought my family life would automatically thrive if I was succeeding at my job. But Jeff taught me to stop thinking excellence will somehow happen and strive to make it happen instead—in *all* areas and relationships that I value.

As I integrated Jeff's ideas on taking the lead, in both my career and at home with my wife and kids, I saw progress in both places. For example, the owner of the accounting firm offered me partner after only three years. Extending this invitation to someone outside his family was something he'd never done and had always said he'd never do.

I was very flattered, but thanks to my conversations with Jeff, I now understood that I had to follow *my* heart and head rather than someone else's vision for my future. Consequently, I chose a position with another company. This made for a sensitive situation interpersonally and careerwise. But Jeff walked me through my exit from the firm in a way that burned no bridges and kept me on track with my goals. And he has talked me through every other major decision of my life since then as:

- I launched and eventually sold my own company.
- My family expanded.
- I joined the New York City office of the company I work

for now (a multinational risk adviser and insurance bro-
kerage that employs forty thousand people worldwide).

• I decided to return to Texas a few years later to assume a
more expanded role with Willis Towers Watson, having
been managing director growth leader, North America,
and now producer.

To his credit, though, Jeff has never given me the answers to my
life. Rather, he's given me the tools I need to keep pursuing new summits as they open up to me.

That's pretty remarkable for someone who has influence in so
many lives. He's mentored literally hundreds of businesspeople within
corporate America and advised thousands of clients during his thirty-
five-plus years with Northwestern. He speaks regularly to adults and
college students across the country. He and his wife, Cindy, have
led in a young marrieds program at one of the largest churches in
America. He teaches an ultrapopular leadership class at Baylor University. He has been on several influential boards, including Baylor
University's Board of Regents. And he is a father of three great kids of
his own. In other words, he has had daily opportunities throughout
his life to *tell* people what to do, or even to say, "Follow me where
I'm going." Instead, he equips others to engage their own plans. He
guides them to discern what is possible for their own gifts and dreams
and relationships, so they can make their possibilities realities.

It took me awhile to catch on to his method. Early in my career,
I so admired Jeff that I thought, *If I emulate this guy, I'll have the
same success and impact he has.* But Jeff doesn't want a bunch of mini-
Reeters running around. In fact, that's the complete opposite of what
he messages to people. And because he has continually reinforced that

idea of "Lead yourself; don't imitate anybody," I rarely consider what others have accomplished anymore. (Including Jeff!) Instead, I set goals according to *my* capabilities, *my* unique design, and *my* capacities. And I've had success I would never have seen had I followed someone else's ideas for me.

That's really at the heart of what Jeff means when he talks about doing life differently in this book. If you don't live by design—by an intentional Master Action Plan that coordinates with how you've specifically been created—you'll end up living by default. A default life leads to boredom, disappointment, and regret. A life by design culminates in dreams fulfilled. Missions accomplished. Obstacles overcome. And opportunities to both lead others *and* show them how to lead themselves.

This is exactly what has happened for me. When I recognized a younger me in twenty-one-year-old Chad, I knew I wanted to invest in him as I'd been invested in. I told him about my mentor, Jeff. And I ventured, "I'd like to help you achieve your goals in a similar way—whether or not you end up with our firm."

Chad joined our company (out of thirty-five college candidates interviewed by our recruiter at four Texas campuses, he was one of only three to whom we offered a position), and he and I were deeply engaged as he learned the ropes in this very demanding, sales-oriented job. He is working hard to pursue his brand of excellence in his endeavors. And even now after he changed jobs, I'm trying to convey to him what I do in my life and work so that he can not only absorb what helps him, but, more importantly, discern for himself what kind of man, husband, father, employee, and leader he's supposed to be.

I'm sure Chad will face some unexpected detours and some

frustrating delays on his life's adventure—we all do. But because Chad has diligently taken inventory of his unique design and dreams, he's living a truth that will carry him as far as he can go. It's also the most important truth of this book, and the one that Jeff Reeter taught me best: *You cannot follow someone else's route to success. Only **you** can lead yourself to the life of uncommon adventure that you were meant to live.*

DO LIFE
DIFFERENTLY

PART ONE

LEAD YOURSELF— CHOOSING A LIFE BY DESIGN

CHAPTER 1

LOST AND FOUND

I was lost. *Really lost.* I just didn't know it yet.

For several hours, I had followed a winding game trail up into the high country of the Uncompahgre National Forest in Colorado. It was an afternoon hunt, and I was unaware that I had made a wrong turn earlier in the day. Consequently, as I hiked and stalked, hoping to find an elusive elk, I'd been distancing myself from our camp all afternoon, heading farther and farther in the opposite direction.

Because wilderness hunts are both a spiritual and physical experience for me, I was far more focused on the excitement of the hunt than on where I was going. *A very rookie mistake.* The mix of colors around me—reds and oranges in the distance at lower elevations, golden-leaved aspens blending with the deep green of firs, and the browns and grays of the rocky ridges as far as my eyes could see—made for a majestic backdrop to this fall adventure.

A little before sundown, I settled in at a scenic spot near a game trail and a small spring. I saw deer but not the prized elk that I sought. Soon, the sun began to disappear past the tops of the western mountains and the air grew noticeably colder, alerting me that it was time to begin hiking back. I geared up, strapped on a headlamp, and pointed myself toward camp. Or so I thought.

The trail was easy to follow, and I moved forward in the graying day at a good pace. Yet the farther I went, the more I realized: *I'm not recognizing any landmarks*. Still, I was confident that if I stuck to the trail, I would soon be joining my hunting buddies for dinner and a couple of rounds of poker before snagging a few hours of sleep prior to tomorrow's hunt.

A mile or two later, the landmarks I was looking for still had not materialized. And my compass wasn't making sense. I knew which direction the sun had set, but suddenly "west" seemed…complicated, and somehow not correct. That's when I reluctantly came to the realization: *I'm lost*.

At that thought, what had been low-level anxiety suddenly spiked, and I did what amateurs do when they get scared: I sped up. To make matters worse, my faster pace caused me to perspire, increasing my risk of hypothermia as the temperature started dropping precipitously in that thin mountain air. My light camouflage clothing was ideal for an active spot-and-stalk hunt during the day, but not for being stranded outdoors overnight in the subfreezing temperatures.

There was another dynamic at work that I am a little embarrassed to share. I like to think of myself as a man's man, with enough nerve to get through any situation. Frankly, though, I was fearful. It felt like the dangers of the unknown were ever present. *Was I the hunter or the hunted?* The noises coming from the shadows worried me; I imagined that a mountain lion or a bear was lurking nearby, ready to maul me at any moment. As much as my reason and intellect told me that those were highly improbable occurrences, they were still in my mind.

To fight the panic and sense of isolation that can easily take over in times like these, I decided I would keep moving, but change directions. The game trail hit a creek bed that led me down the mountain. This seemed a favorable sign. Yet I couldn't help regretting an earlier decision. The dates for the trip had been selected, in part, so that we could hunt on a week with very little moonlight (elk tend to be more active during the day when there is a "lesser" moon at night). *How I would love to have a little of that moonlight now!* I thought as darkness overtook the dusk. Thankfully, the clouds above me shifted at one point, allowing me to see the Big Dipper and its spout, which always points to the North Star. Once I located that, I was able to make sense of my compass readings and regain my bearings. And just a little way farther, the creek bed crossed a dirt road.

I was feeling relieved until I came face-to-face with my next dilemma: I didn't know which way to go on the road. After consulting my compass again, I picked a direction and kept walking at a steady pace, trying to keep my body temperature up. Finally, well into the wee morning hours, a local in an older white pickup truck drove by. I desperately waved him down and told him I was lost. He offered me a ride and I climbed in, gratefully soaking in the warmth from the truck's heater as we chatted.

"I'm amazed you got to where you did on foot," he said when I told him where our camp was. Knowing the entire area as he did, he drove me safely back to our site, where I found my buddies soundly sleeping, not at all concerned for my safety!

LEARNING TO LEAD

Looking back on the early years of my high-mountain hunting adventures, it's a wonder I didn't get lost more often. I was pretty clueless—there's just no other way to say it. I had some knowledgeable friends I hunted with, I'd gone hunting with my dad and brother for years, and I regularly read books and magazines on stalking techniques, but generally speaking, I saw scattered success because I didn't know how to guide myself. I hadn't yet had the privilege of going on a guided hunt, either.

Once I began taking professionally guided hunts, my knowledge grew by leaps and bounds. Most of the time I learned things *to* do, and some of the time I learned things *not* to do, to be successful. And the differences between myself in that early experience in Colorado and those top elk-hunting guides in their expertise have become more and more apparent. There is nothing haphazard about their approach.

They remain keenly aware of the objectives. Yes, one of those is to provide a fun, productive hunt for their clients. But a safe return to camp is the other, so that no one is unnecessarily put in harm's way.

Their steps are strategic.

They are constantly checking their compasses and tracking our position.

They monitor the terrain, the skies, and the horizon for any signs of trouble.

They note wind direction and observe temperature changes.

They listen and watch for signs of animal activity, analyzing how to move us from a good location to a better one, and from better to best.

They gauge our distance ahead of time and adjust our pace as needed so we can make camp before our resources are depleted.

They move more slowly when it matters and move more briskly (but quietly) when it doesn't. Strangely, they listen to the stillness and find direction. Distinctively and differently, they quietly and faithfully position us for success.

As I've grown older and added several guided hunts to my experience, I've also—thanks to the training and example of these guides—learned to lead myself. To make my steps count. To determine ahead of time where I want to go and plan for it. To be a stronger observer of my surroundings. To know my strengths and weaknesses so I can maximize whatever situations the wilderness presents me with and enjoy even greater success in my pursuits.

I've also discovered I don't want to stop there. Said another way, successful hunts are no longer my end goal. I strive to make every trip its own adventure, pushing myself to pursue greater goals, create richer memories, build deeper connections with my traveling companions, and gain further insight into who I am and why I'm doing the things I do.

This, in essence, encapsulates my intentions for my life, too. As I've learned to lead myself out in the wilderness, I've sought to apply those lessons elsewhere—to my life and heart. I am determined not to be a default dad who lets his sons raise themselves, hoping they turn out okay. Not to default to poor habits, expecting my body to stay healthy on its own. I don't want to be the kind of guy who, as Jeff Turner said in the foreword to this book, is a wild success at work but leaves a neglected wife in his wake. I want the most I can get out of this one life I have. That means doing everything possible to not only set and succeed at lofty goals but to pursue the loftiest outcome of all: a life of significance where I'm also serving others with my time and gifts. I call it pursuing "Life at its BEST." BEST is an acronym for Balance, Excellence, Service, Truth. Over thirty years ago, my coach and friend, Jack Shaw, and I developed this concept, and we've been seeking to live it and teach it ever since.

In your heart of hearts, I suspect that's what you long for, too, even if you've kind of given up hope that it can happen. I'm wagering that no matter your current situation—whether you've seen some success or not, whether you've lost your way or maybe never found it in the first place—you still wish for greatness. You want a great career, a great family, greater wealth, greater purpose, greater impact, and greater faith.

TEST YOURSELF

Let's test this. You walk into a room, and you see this word written on a whiteboard in black marker:

ORDINARY

How does the word *ordinary* make you feel? What do you visualize?

When I ask a roomful of people the same questions, it doesn't matter what anyone's age or income or relationship status is; the answers are immediate and pretty much the same:

"I don't want to be ordinary!"

"It's just so…vanilla and boring."

"There's nothing remarkable about it."

"But ordinary is normal!" I respond. "That's what most people claim to be happy with!" Then we start to apply this term to areas of significant meaning: "Ordinary spouse," I say. "What's an ordinary spouse?" After hearing some answers, I sum it up with, "Whether I am an ordinary spouse or I am married to an ordinary spouse, that setup works pretty well for maybe seven or eight years—until somebody throws in the towel with divorce papers."

Next, we move on to ordinary health. "One number comes to my mind at this lack of sustained activity," I say. "The number sixty-six—the average age of a first heart attack among American men. Is that okay with you?"

After we go through a few more key examples, the room will claim, "Ordinary is not okay. Ordinary is normal, and I want more than that!"

"Okay, then," I challenge, "what if we add something to it?" With a bright-colored marker, I write five letters in all caps at the front of the word.

"That's it!" they'll exclaim. They want to be **EXTRA**ordinary.

And that's what I'm counting on in this book. That in your heart of hearts, you don't want to be an ordinary spouse or an average parent or an everyday single with a job that bores you and a life that empties you. You want that something extra. Something more compelling, energizing, and stimulating that draws you out of bed each day and propels you to engage your heart and mind in everything you do.

I'm also pretty sure that you don't like being lost any more than I do. Yes, we all get off track sometimes in our lives and lose our way. I can get lost on any given day in my life because of pridefulness, lack of focus, or failing to effectively value another person. Still, I have three goals for myself and for you:

1. that we get lost a little less;

2. that when we're lost, we still navigate forward effectively using life systems we can depend on; and

3. that we wholeheartedly plan and engage in the kind of life pursuit that captivates us and inspires those we influence.

If you're on board for *EXTRAordinary*, then you have to be willing to be atypical. Uncommon. A bit radical, as in willing to go beyond the status quo. Because people who lead themselves are different. They do life differently on a strategic path toward extraordinary. At some point, they decide to step away from the crowd and do what others aren't willing to do.

You simply can't be the same as everybody you know if you're intent on leading yourself and achieving significance. This is a road less traveled, a distinctive journey packed with uncommon adventures, fantastic summits, and a spectacular ending that continues to be felt long after we're gone.

Not everyone dares to travel apart from the pack. But those who want more from their lives do. Those who want to lead others do. As one reporter wrote: "People become leaders in stages and gain essential skills at each turn. First, they learn to lead themselves, then to lead others."[1] They prepare so that when change is needed, and people are crying out for someone to show them the way, they're ready. They've already learned their purpose, and they're going hard after it. They're maximizing their giftedness and resources. They've tightened up their habits. They've dreamed big things and developed a bold vision that is progressively coming true. In essence, they can assume the lead because they've practiced leading themselves first.

Take a moment to process this. I'm challenging *you* to be abnormal. Out of the ordinary. To most of the people you know, not being normal is a truly scary proposition. Yet the road less traveled, as poet Robert Frost wrote, is the one that makes all the difference. I'm so hopeful you'll see the difference as you read through this book.

You will have to lead yourself to live distinctively, intentionally, and according to your unique purpose, but as you do, amazing vistas will spread out before you. You will reach many summits and plant many seeds. And in the end, you will have made a difference, a legacy, a life for yourself and for the generations to come.

This is what it means to attain significance, and *this* is what we'll be training for in the pages that follow. The secret is to rise up and lead yourself according to your one-of-a-kind design, not according to the "designs"—the expectations or plans—of others.

Maybe your role models didn't teach you how to set measurable goals.

Maybe you have no clue about which habits will make you thrive.

Maybe there are so many voices speaking into your life that you can't locate your own.

Maybe aspirations such as "living your dreams" and "reaching significance" seem as beyond your capacity as summiting Mount Everest.

If any of those "maybes" describe you, I'd like to be one of your guides. Not because I've figured it all out, but because I had others who showed me how to lead myself, and I've both seen and felt what a difference it has made as I've applied their expertise. That's what I want for you as well.

It's a lifelong process; we will *always* need to be leading ourselves if we're going to strive beyond mere success and aim higher as spouses, parents, businesspeople, and citizens. But I'm on that trail, and I want you to join me so that you can find not just success but significance, too.

This isn't about me telling you who you are and what to do. You have to be you and take your own path, not follow Jeff Reeter's route. I'm here to help you plan and think your way through for yourself.

On your trail will be many surprises. The goal is to equip you to live *your* uncommon adventure, figuring out what empowers you. What triggers your courage. What sustains and motivates you. And most of all, what you really want from your time on this earth so you can maximize the journey you're on.

My wife and I just got back from a mountain hike on a snowy day. It was a chilly, brisk adventure. We walked up the trail for a ways before the snow got so deep we couldn't go any farther. Thankfully, we had packed snowshoes, so Cindy and I strapped them on and continued our outing. The snowmelt above us caused the brook along our trail to rush with rapids and waterfalls. It was majestic and invigorating. We experienced the thrill of accomplishment (and some incredible scenery) on our journey.

This little outing of ours is a microcosm of the life adventure that I believe is available to each of us. We're on a path we have chosen, alongside companions we have chosen. Though the trail forward is somewhat unknown, and the conditions are not always ideal, our preparedness greatly affects the success of the outing.

BY DESIGN, NOT DEFAULT

At the end of the day, doing life differently is about living by design, not by default. It's about making life happen rather than letting life happen to you. Very simply: *it's about YOU leading YOU based on your unique ability.*

That's what makes this book different. Countless books focus on leadership. (I have several shelves full of them myself!) Numerous podcasts and TED Talks speak about leading others, leading organizations, developing leaders, and so on. There are far fewer books on the importance of leading ourselves with bold vision and carefully considered life systems. And yet, before you can lead others well, much less discover real success or leave a legacy that others will remember you for, you must first learn to lead yourself.

This book is about you leading yourself, again and again, through the many adventures that life presents you with. It's about you leading you whenever you're lost and afraid. You leading you to get unstuck every time *stuck* happens. You leading you to track down your greatness. And, this may surprise you, but it's also about you leading your own fight against the gravitational pull of average to powerfully pursue what matters most in your heart of hearts.

What's wrong with default? What's wrong with being like everybody else? Nothing—except that "good is the enemy of great," as author Jim Collins says.[2] Logically, then, ordinary is the enemy of extraordinary. Settling by default for an average life means following the crowd, which means relinquishing the opportunity to achieve more, impact more people, and live your life to the fullest.

As a financial adviser, I've asked literally thousands of people: "In the next three years, what are your goals personally, professionally, and financially?" Most of them had none to start with, but as we worked through their ideals with great *intention*, and paid real *attention* to their individual designs, I watched person after person lead themselves out of any "wilderness," any tragedy or circumstance, to greater levels of success and significance. This was done by purposefully walking through uncommon adventures to their finish, by making very specific plans to succeed, and, most meaningfully, by making choices to serve and impact others, not just themselves.

I've been pursuing this kind of intentionality for over three decades. But here's something critical for you to know: I am truly just a *normal guy*. My family moved around quite a bit when I was a kid, but I considered Jenks, Oklahoma—the heartland of Middle America—home. How in the world I arrived at some of the places I've been makes no sense, except maybe that I've had my fair share of good influences and mentors in my life, and I've tried to pay attention to them.

The reason I'm sharing this with you is that if a dude like me can do some of the things I've done, then I'm absolutely certain you can do plenty of extraordinary things, too. It's important to give yourself a chance, because your entire experience on this earth depends on your daily decisions between "default" and "design." You can be led by others, by the happenstance of circumstance…or you can saddle up and take the reins for yourself.

YOUR LIFE, YOUR LEAD

It's your life to lead. Will you go for it? I'll be right there with you, offering specific tools and training so that you can identify not only where you are but where you want to be, plus the action steps for getting there. I'll also help you very practically apply guiding principles in the areas that seem to matter to most people: work, finances, health, relationships, and faith. This way, you can determine what *you* need to lead yourself, step-by-step and turn-by-turn, from survival to success to significance.

It will be up to you to customize what you learn, since your particular route will be uniquely yours. But I'll help set you up with the vision and understanding you'll need to reach the summits that could be in your sights. I'll also present numerous ideas for integrating your goals, your values, your beliefs, and your habits day by day to create a life and legacy you can be proud of. *The* life and legacy you're specially meant to live.

At its essence, leading yourself is what gives life to your individual dreams and purpose during your time on this planet. It means setting your sights on things that excite you, and conquering the challenges and reaching the horizons that you alone were designed for, with confidence. It means taking inventory of everything within you and around you so that you can find your way toward the top of the mountain and not stay lost or continually wander. And mostly, it means devising a system for how to live to the fullest in your work, your relationships, and your finances so that maybe, just maybe, you'll reach the summits you've had your eye on.

CHAPTER 2

DEFAULT OR DESIGN? YOUR CRITICAL CHOICE

You might be surprised to learn that while I was lost in the Colorado forest, I actually had a map with me. It was a "topo"—topographical—map, which shows permanent natural landmarks such as mountain ranges, forests, and waterways, as well as man-made ones (roads and railways, existing buildings, etc.). Outdoorsmen use this kind of map to get an aerial view of a specific area's terrain so they can chart a course that will accomplish their purposes. Whether for a leisurely hike through great scenery, or finding prime hunting or camping spots, the topo allows them to choose their best route from the comfort of home, long before they ever set foot in remote territory.

So how did I get lost? I mean, I had my map and compass with me, and I knew how to use them. I also knew where our base camp was on the topo. What happened with me? For several hours on that day, I was a walking illustration of living by default. You might say I went on autopilot out there.

For one, I didn't plot my route all the way through to the finish. The things I *had* done in advance of that day's hunt are probably what allowed me to eventually find my way out, but it was a major mistake for me to charge up that mountain without a plan that would bring me to the successful completion of that adventure.

Second, I didn't reference my guides along the way. I wasn't in the habit of following them. Once I was actually on the trail, I quit paying attention to those guides and neglected to use any of my resources. It was almost sundown before I tried to make heads or tails of my location, and that was way too late.

Only when I "woke up" to my surroundings and the dilemma I was in did I start leading myself out of danger.

THE DANGER OF DEFAULT

Have you had a similar experience in your travels? You believed everything was okay until darkness descended, and then it hit you: "Oh no, I'm not where I thought I was." Or you were just driving along on cruise control, oblivious, and suddenly, upon returning your attention to the road, you wondered, "Did I miss my exit? I have no idea how I got here!"

Sadly, for anyone who is living by default in their journey through life, these aren't just occasional incidents. Losing their way is common. Autopilot has become almost second nature. Disorientation and uncertainty are familiar feelings. People keep ending up in places they never anticipated—detached from their job or spouse, quietly disappointed in their financial situation or spiritual life, falling short in their career or physical fitness—without knowing why.

To never awaken to your situation is troubling enough; it causes stress and instability for you and for everyone who relies on you, from family to friends to the people you work with. Yet there's a greater danger: if you never open your eyes and determine to lead yourself out of that situation, what should have been a passing *circumstance* can quickly become a *condition*—something more permanent, a way of life even.

Many people are where they are by default, not design. They're idling or creeping along in low gear rather than using all their horsepower. My failure to lead myself from start to finish on my hunting trip cost me some anxiety and a few lost hours. Failing to lead yourself throughout your life can cost far more. It can waylay your dreams and the one-of-a-kind impact you are supposed to have.

A DESIGN FOR YOUR LIFE

Trust me, there's no judgment here. Most people have never been taught to take inventory and set goals that fit who they are and what they want out of life. I learned this in my financial-services practice. For several years, I sat down with at least fifteen people per week and talked about their lives, their goals, and their visions. Today, I'm privileged to lead an incredible firm with over fifty thousand clients in various socioeconomic situations. Using a carefully developed process, these clients have been equipped to define their financial goals, devise strategies suited to their families and their lifestyles, and make their dreams a reality—and they're doing it! One day, one step, one goal at a time.

This is essentially what you will be doing in this book…but for your *life*, not just your finances. You'll take yourself from wishing to fulfillment, fully engaged in maximizing every adventure God has you on. Whatever you believe about the existence of a higher power—or don't—is fine. I personally believe that our lives are a gift from our Creator God, and that He wants to help us on our journey. In any case, if you'll carefully explore who you are, by the time you've come to the last page of this book, you'll be well on your way to leading yourself to the destiny you've been created for.

Where's the path to that kind of outcome? How do you determine the course you should take? By design.

THE BIG DEAL ABOUT DESIGN

I read somewhere that "the best way to predict the future is to create it."[1] When I refer to living *by design*, I do mean purposefully and mindfully leading yourself to create your future. I also mean doing so according to how you've singularly been created, according to *your* distinct design and purpose.

This involves taking inventory of all the aspects of your unique, God-given design *and* using its markers—your passions, opportunities, experiences, intentions, skills, and talents—as compass points to intentionally chart (or design) a clear course to each of your dreams. You also want to pay attention to how everything about you is working together and aiming you toward your highest goals, your best self.

To live so mindfully equates to leading yourself. And leading yourself is what enables you to achieve tremendous results. You not only see greater success—attaining your personal goals—but you also get to fulfill your purpose, forging some really cool paths that no one else has ever traveled and impacting people in ways that no one else ever will.

Summarizing the beliefs of leadership guru Warren Bennis, Rob Asghar wrote that "most people who become good leaders don't set out to become leaders. They simply set out to become *themselves*, in an authentic manner. And they deploy every means at their disposal toward that end."[2] Truly, we find our greatest successes and significance in leading ourselves to live by design *because we have been designed*. In detail. Right down to our very molecules. Our fingerprints are unique to us; our life print should be as well.

We are all fearfully and wonderfully made, fashioned to do extraordinary things. Translation: there's absolutely nothing "ordinary" about any of us ordinary folk…except when we opt to live by default. Were you really to take stock of your blessings—from the body you have, to your gifts, the capacity of your mind, your network of relationships, and the world of opportunities before you—the evidence would be overwhelming: you are capable of leading yourself to do exceedingly above and beyond what you could ever fathom. Do you hear that? You can and should follow through on those next-level dreams and plans. But you won't if you're invested in keeping to what's familiar. Making no waves. Blending in and following the crowd.

A SOCIAL EPIDEMIC

For all of our supposedly distinct online profiles and pages, we live in a society that actually doesn't like to stray too far from center. I sometimes say that our culture seeks to be homogenized. Merriam-Webster says to be homogenized is to be made uniform or similar. I am convinced that we are actually meant to thrive in our uniqueness. In our world today, we are doing worse and worse at embracing differences. In reality, though, our differences and uniqueness add the spice of life that can truly matter. Somebody else's perspective or life experience that is different from mine can be the difference between ordinary and extraordinary. Our financial-services firm does extensive testing when interviewing prospective advisers as candidates for that career. Those tests magically show us the uniqueness of each individual, and that they are fearfully, wonderfully, and individually fashioned to be their most powerful selves. If our firm does what it ought to do, we help them thrive in their uniqueness, rather than homogenize them toward sameness.

Make no mistake: when we strive for no differences among us, we are living by default, and *default = survival*. That may seem a presumptuous statement, but my conversations with so many clients and trainees about the status of their lives has convinced me of this fundamental fact.

Lots of people are blind to it, and they don't call it that. Still, scores of men and women, young adults, and teens are living by default every day, acclimating themselves to the status quo and thus to survival. They may not be completely lost, but they're operating without a plan, unaware of their purpose, and oblivious to their higher calling and the gifts of their uniqueness. They've settled for "average," "normal," and "the comfort of the crowd" rather than leading themselves to new frontiers.

I met with one of our team's aspiring leaders recently, and he's doing pretty well for himself. Though he often needs coaching, I recognize that he is powerful in ways that he has trouble seeing. What concerns me is that he seems to like "familiar." His familiar is normal. And he sure doesn't want to be different.

This young man doesn't know it yet, but that one fear of his—the fear of being seen as different—is a greater threat to his future than almost anything that could actually happen to him. Should an obvious crisis come, he'll probably fight to overcome it. But he doesn't view ordinary as a problem, much less a disease. He doesn't consider *average* to be terminal in any way. And yet it absolutely is. It ruins our dreams and robs us of our futures.

It doesn't take much to fall victim to this epidemic that has infected our society, our schools, our souls. This condition is so insidious that, whether you follow the crowd *because* it's normal, or you *default* to following the crowd over following your own dreams and plans, this one "social disease" can chronically and persistently sideline you. To never step away from the crowd and breathe the fresh air of an uncommon adventure is to eventually take yourself out of the game for good.

The antidote I recommend is this: quit defaulting to whatever person or group you've been relying on outside yourself. It's one thing to look to God for the kind of guidance only He can give, but on a human level, you have to look inside yourself before you look to other people.

Your greatest impact will come from learning to lead yourself first. "Whether you flounder or flourish is always in your hands—you are the single biggest *human* influence in your life," says Oprah Winfrey. "Your journey begins with a choice to get up, step out, and live fully."[3] So, if you're feeling that pull to follow the crowd, let me urge you: don't!

Don't be that person who never steps out due to fear, or who passively waits things out.

Don't be the wandering soul who casually tags along behind your friends.

As important as I feel it is to vote, is someone different in DC or your statehouse really going to make *your* life better? No. The world needs the leader *in the center of your chest.*

Your calling demands it.

Your family longs for it.

Your circle of influence expects it.

Your colleagues and community are crying out for it.

Kurt Russell, portraying Olympic hockey coach Herb Brooks in the movie *Miracle*, told the team in one particularly powerful scene: "This cannot be a team of common men, because common men go nowhere. You have to be uncommon." That's true of us individually, too.

Why don't *you* become an agent of change? Powerfully pursue uncommon impact in your neighborhood, your faith community, your city, your world. Decide: *I will not be relegated to some small pursuit. There is important work to be done, and I am the one to do it.*

DEFINING *DEFAULT*

I am convinced that while many people live average lives, most of them don't want to. Not if they really thought about it. Everybody follows the crowd when they're not thinking about it. But those who are mindful won't.

Mindfulness is one of the things that distinguish those who lead themselves. The dictionary says that to live *by default* is "to revert automatically either to a preselected option or to something that is standard or familiar." To me, that's a telling description. Those who live by default are inclined to "revert," or go back to, either what they've known or what everyone else does—in effect, moving away from their dreams. They're also inclined to do this "automatically," as in without thinking and without considering other options.

I've already referred to default as being on autopilot. It's that cruise control, "set it and forget it" mentality where you're just along for the ride rather than really navigating the route. You're letting life happen and expecting things to work out. If that's you, if you've assumed that "success comes to those who wait," and you're happy to keep hanging out, you're living in the defeat of default.

Default takes many forms, but it is most evident in passive patterns such as:

- settling for "good enough" rather than going for "great";
- surrendering your goals to fit in;
- thinking that something else has to happen first (marriage, children, buying a house, having every detail in place) before you can pursue the life you want;
- laziness; and
- ignoring matters of the heart.

Living by default also shows in our immediate reactions to stress, such as:

- choosing to stay put when you get stuck;
- giving up after a failure;

- heading for home as soon as an obstacle presents itself or someone opposes you; and
- seeking shortcuts.

Where did you find yourself on this list? How many of these patterns or reactions are almost instinctual to you?

If you discovered that you have been living by default in even a few areas, don't be discouraged. Realizing where you've lost your way is a move toward living by design and advancing toward your dreams. We will talk about practical steps for situations exactly like these in future chapters.

NO CASUALTIES

Admittedly, even when you do everything right, you can still sometimes end up in the wrong place. My concern in these pages, however, is that you not become a "wilderness casualty"—someone who gets off course and never finds their way out of the woods. I'd love to see you not only find your way out of danger, but also go on to excel in every adventure and conquer every mountain you're capable of conquering. In other words, I don't want you to miss out on *anything* great that should have been a part of your life's journey!

Tragically, some of the people you know *will* lose out on their dreams because they lack a vision and a plan for activating it. Others will forgo making their mark because they tried to follow someone else's lead rather than leading themselves. Many more will miss out on mountaintop views because they opted to stay below with the crowd rather than climb to where eagles soar. Only a few will ever enjoy their destiny and fulfill their purpose.

Anyone *could*, mind you; we've all been given the potential to go big, choose better, complete our goals, and make a real and lasting difference for others. But most won't.

You will, however, by committing to the exploration and pursuit of your very best. I'm talking about *your* best, not your mentor's or your spouse's best; not your boss's or your hero's best. Yours will look different from everyone else's. After all, as the only you who's ever been born, you're striving to become the best *you*, not the second-best version of somebody else.

There's nothing wrong with admiring the genius of Steve Jobs, the wealth of Warren Buffett, or the worldwide platform of Oprah Winfrey, or the Fixer Upper creativity of Chip and Joanna Gaines— we can and should take lessons from others who have preceded us. Pay attention, though, to the real secret behind their success. What's the difference between these high achievers and most people? *They designed the life they wanted and went for it, full throttle.* They didn't wait for it. They didn't sit around hoping it would just happen somehow. They didn't cater to the crowd or demand ideal circumstances before taking action. And, if you know their stories, they certainly weren't deterred by difficulty or opposition. Each one of them recognized their distinctive strengths, maximized their potential, combined their passions with a vision, and wholeheartedly pursued a plan to fulfill their dreams.

So can you.

It's not being selfish; it's smart. You're learning to think ahead and think beyond yourself at the same time. Not just in an effort to enhance your own life experience but to enrich the lives of others.

Selfishness is the easiest of defaults—it's so second nature, we don't have to think about it! But such pursuits also keep us stuck.

Our thinking, our routines, our relationships…nothing ever gets much better when we're overly centered on "self." To lead yourself, on the other hand, is to set your sights further and higher, not only on worthwhile goals but on big causes and impassioned service to others as well. Selflessness is what truly moves you toward greatness. Not the greatness of celebrity, but the greatness of directing yourself toward lasting pursuits that will change others' lives.

LEADING WITH PURPOSE

Plenty of people in this world want to lead. They want to be in charge, simply because they like the idea of having control. "In a sense…," says journalist Rob Asghar, "the modern leadership-industrial complex is catering to…ambitious people who crave influence and authority, but who may not have any meaningful use for that influence and authority."[4] Warren Bennis, however, understood the calling as well as anyone: "A leader is not simply someone who experiences the personal exhilaration of being in charge. A leader is someone whose actions have the most profound consequences on other people's lives…sometimes forever and ever."[5] Contrary to what our culture trumpets, you don't need position, fame, or fortune to design a life of such impact. You just need to know how to lead yourself—and do it.

One of the secret benefits of living by design is that, in the big picture, what anybody else accomplishes doesn't affect your ability to accomplish just as much or more. Your heroes or role models have led themselves to the heights they could reach; you're leading yourself to the heights you can reach. You're going places that those people will never get to see. You're influencing people with whom those people will never have an audience. You may be an "ordinary" person as the world perceives it, but you were made to do extraordinary things. You have the capacity, the calling, and the capability to go deeper and higher than wherever you are now, and probably far beyond what you've let yourself imagine, by taking the lead in your own life.

Leading yourself in this way, with powerful clarity and intention, is critical to life success. And because you don't know what tomorrow will bring, you want a strategy that is multifaceted, one that purposefully prepares you for sustained growth. It should help you build character, perseverance, wisdom, and habits that you can draw on when you need to step it up as a spouse, a boss, an employee, a citizen, a parent, a son, or a daughter. This, in essence, is what defines the individual who has learned to live by design. It's someone who strives to be all they can be, so that they are at their very best every time they need to be. Or, as I spontaneously put it in a talk to our firm a couple of months after my father passed away: "Who are you going to be, when you need to be who you need to be?"

Your life adventure is truly "mission critical," and as soon as you understand this, you'll be on your way. By "mission critical," I mean you are here for a reason. You have been endowed with a specially designated purpose that sets you apart from every other human being. That purpose will have many expressions—many callings—across the seasons of your life, but discovering what you're here for will catapult you to maximum effectiveness and impact.

Where can you best serve the world and others? How do you exercise your uniqueness to achieve your ultimate purpose? These are the kinds of questions you will be exploring in the chapters ahead. But first, make the critical choice to accept this all-important mission of leading yourself to live by design, not default.

NOTES FROM MY JOURNEY

We all get off course sometimes, including those who are living by design. So, how do we reroute ourselves? How can we quickly recalculate and get back on track as our GPS helps us do? Here are some basic coordinates that have kept me headed in the right direction in times when my specific path was uncertain.

Prepare for what you can. Survival guides always talk about how critical preparation is. They emphasize the need to plan for the worst while expecting the best. My dad used to say, "Failing to plan is planning to fail." For our purpose here, it is a must to think through the importance of preparing for a life adventure. And why not? Many of us spend months planning for an annual vacation, wanting to make sure it's extraordinary. Should we spend less time planning for an extraordinary life?

Do all you can with all you have. Those who learn to lead themselves not only prepare for what's ahead, they also make the most of everything at their disposal, whether it's little or much. Maybe you haven't yet taken inventory, but there are four necessities for every traveler—and you already possess each one:

1. You carry a fire inside you. That fire is your *passions.* A few years ago, while sitting at a blazing firepit at our ranch, I coined the phrase, "Live life by the heart of the fire." Some people go to their grave without ever tapping into what excites them, but the sooner you do, the quicker you'll progress. Your will, your heart, and your mind always find a way when you know what you love and you're earnestly pursuing it.

2. You have been given particular *skills* and *strengths* that will advance you toward your goals. You may not have a ton of talents, but you have the ones you need to top the mountains you're meant to climb. You may be young, but what experience you do have, you can build on. Your abilities, just like your muscles, can be trained and strengthened. Don't overlook what you have within you just because somebody else has a different skill set than you.

3. We all take certain *provisions* with us, both equipment and supplies. Suppose yours isn't the best travel gear that money can buy because funds are limited. Suppose it's only a partial list of stuff that survival experts recommend for hiking through unknown territory. Are you doomed? Not at all. You may just have to work a little harder to lead yourself.

4. You have your *guides*—among them, your internal compass, your faith, and your traveling companions. Each of these provides an important and reliable reference point by which you can make wise decisions every step of the way, staying the course toward significance. My best daily guide is my wife, Cindy. She has great wisdom and insightful intuition. Also, I'm blessed with some college fraternity brothers who are like true brothers. They serve as good guides for me, too.

Pursue your dreams, not someone else's. You're the best person to discern how you've been designed and, with that in mind, to design your own life. You never want somebody else to decide it for you. Not your dad, your mom, your boss, or that guy or girl you'd like to impress.

Go after what's best, not just what's good. Everyone is capable of a certain level of life success, even if they're not living by their unique design and purpose. If you think about it, a ballpoint pen can be used to some effect as a nail, but its best and highest use is as what its creator intended: a writing instrument. I want you to call yourself higher—to your best self, not just your getting-by self—so that you visualize what you want, and then you get it. You plan for it, and you make it happen. It's a matter of recognizing that everything in life entails a good, a better, and a best, and then choosing best.

Pursue the right things for the right reasons. The perks of success are often a by-product of pursuing one's passions. So, don't ever let your end goal be material things; people who do are automatically limiting themselves. If you seek first to serve and love, to matter and make a difference, to be a catalyst in the lives of others…you providentially end up with some pretty extraordinary outcomes. Meanwhile, you open the doors—and the eyes of your mind and heart—to what is possible.

CHAPTER 3

THE SIGNIFICANCE OF SIGNIFICANCE

Alan Arnette is a former high-tech business executive who made three attempts on Mount Everest before summiting at age fifty-four. Since his first mountaintop experience on Mont Blanc in his late thirties, he has continued to challenge himself because he admittedly enjoys going after goals he sets for himself. Now, though, he also spends his time preparing other adventurers for their climbs. Calling himself the "Summit Coach," his marketing slogan pretty much says it all: "You're about to…climb the mountain of your dreams—but are you ready?"[1]

I'm similarly invested in you and your dreams throughout this book. Like Mr. Arnette, I, too, want you to be ready to climb in order to have the journey of a lifetime. The mountains I'm talking about, however, are mountains that encompass the mind and heart. And I'm not referring to just one mountaintop, but many. Not just this year's adventures, but numerous adventures for as long as you live.

Just as with every summit climb, preparation is essential for every individual's lead-yourself journey. In this chapter, I'll introduce you to each of the levels you must progress through to reach your destiny. We'll then discuss some of the need-to-knows about the three levels, to train you for what to expect as you begin your journey out of default and toward your next—or possibly your first—uncommon adventure.

THE CHALLENGE

There's a reason I am so intent on helping individuals lead themselves from default to a life by design: I hate to see people who are perfectly capable of an extraordinary existence (i.e., you, me, and everyone we know) settling for less. We were made to "fire on all cylinders," so to speak—to aim high and achieve those aims—and deep inside we sense it. However, I don't think most of us have stopped to consider what living at this elevated existence looks like, or the dangers of settling in at a less desirable place. To think of the lead-yourself journey as a high-mountain climb can help us get the picture.

By any definition, Mount Everest is considered the peak of all peaks on earth. As such, it has become a trendy site among would-be adventurers from all over the world. Between thirty thousand and forty thousand people a year travel to Everest in search of an epic experience, the vast majority of them amateur climbers.

According to various sources, about 90 percent of those many thousands of travelers will go only so far as base camp. A few thousand will make it farther up the mountain, but never get to savor the views from what is literally the top of our world. On average, less than seven hundred determined climbers (not counting their Sherpa guides) will have the peak experience and reach Everest's 29,029-foot summit.

The peak knows no prejudice. Although the average age of the big-mountain climbers tends to be thirties and forties, people of all ages and experience levels have made it to the top. The youngest? An eighth-grade boy from California and a teenage Nepalese girl. The oldest? An eighty-year-old man from Japan and a woman in her seventies, also from Japan. While almost everyone who goes to Everest each year lives to tell about it, a few adventurers do lose their lives, and a small percentage walk away with permanent injuries.

Similarly, in the lead-yourself journey, anyone can go for the top—you don't have to fit certain criteria or be an expert "climber." But the only ones who ever make it all the way up are the ones who try. The biggest crowd remains at the bottom and never goes any further.

AT BASE LEVEL

The Everest base camp in particular is a microcosm of the first level of any lead-yourself adventure, and one of Arnette's YouTube videos from April 2016 captures it well.

Here are some of my impressions from what he filmed, along with a few facts:

The first thing that greets the eye is how crowded the base camp is. There are sleeping tents of every size and color for as far as the camera's eye can see, and multicolored prayer flags whipping in the Everest winds. Large cooking, dining, and communication tents are in one location, along with showers that had propane-heated water. From this side of Everest, the summit is visible, and it looks majestic and fearsome at the same time. Yet the foot of the mountain is so overpopulated that you notice the chaos before you notice the grandeur of the view above you.

The tents sit atop the constantly shifting Khumbu Icefall. Sprawling about a mile wide in jagged tiers, the base camp on this day houses thirty-two climbing teams representing approximately fifty countries— roughly one thousand people in all between Sherpas, camp personnel, and intended climbers.

Along the periphery of the camp is a small mountain stream with hard-flowing water that must be double-boiled before drinking. Fresh food is brought in every day by porters and yaks from the lower villages. As Arnette pans across the rugged terrain, people can be seen tending fires, preparing meals, checking their gear, or drinking coffee in the food tent. A number of hopeful climbers are sitting around, visiting with one another as they acclimate.[2]

Life at this level isn't fancy by any means. But there's enough here with which to make do should a person decide to stick around.

In life, just as in the actual wilderness, *survival* is the first and base level of existence. The primary concerns are food, shelter, clothing, and fire, not growth or conquest. As long as you hang out here, you may be getting by, but you're not thriving. Not improving. And not advancing toward the next level. In the context of leading yourself, think of it as being distant from who you were created to be and what you were designed to be doing. You were made to achieve uncommon and extraordinary things, but for any number of reasons, you're not. At least not yet.

Often when I ask clients, mentees, or trainees to describe their lives, the ones who have acclimated to this level initially tell me: "Things are fine…Everything's pretty normal." But the more we talk, the more they begin to admit, "I feel lost…stuck…bored. I'm not happy. My marriage isn't that great…My work doesn't fulfill me." What I also hear from many of them is that they really do want to shoot for the top and see their dreams fulfilled, but something (and that *something* is different for everybody) is keeping them from trying for that next level.

Missing Something?

When we aren't vigorously engaged in the pursuit of our goals at the highest levels, it's common to feel dissatisfied, as if we're missing something. The truth is, we *are* missing something, but probably not what we assume.

People who are living by default associate survival with scarcity. In their minds, survival is that dangerous place where a person lacks protection, resources, or help. Though life at this level does entail heightened vulnerability, people in every era in history—in wartime, in famine, in times of persecution and prejudice—have found ways to lead themselves and live by design in spite of minimal support or resources. So, the real danger is not in what we don't have. The threat at this level is fear, and what it can do to a person's hopes and dreams.

When you're in survival mode, and especially when you're mired in default thinking, it can feel like you have everything to lose by taking a risk and leaving base camp. But that's fear talking, not the truth. You were designed for significance, not mere survival. Defeating your fears will help you get there.

Where Fear Looms Largest

It's possible to feel fear at any of the three levels, but it looms largest in the territory of survival (probably because we're at the base of the mountain looking up). Wherever fear looms, we are prone to see only with our eyes, not with our hearts. And before we know it, our dreams have vanished into thin air.

This is where most people falter. This is what keeps most people down. We are all too quick to back off of our desires and settle for the safety of certainty before we've even given ourselves a chance at something better. And though we may not be thriving where we are, we have a remarkable ability to console ourselves with thoughts like, *At least I kind of know what to expect here. It's not really that bad.*

I've heard it described as "my familiar"—a comfortable place. Some people actually claim to enjoy living in a tent for weeks at a time, huddled among a crowd of people! Yet familiarity doesn't change the facts: you're still in a state of survival, sitting at the base of what was supposed to be a really great, high-mountain adventure… going nowhere. In this earliest stage of leading yourself, I encourage you not only to step up, out of survival and into something new, but to step out—away from the crowd—to forge your own trail.

I understand that we're often reluctant to change. Especially at base camp, it's common to perceive safety in numbers and console ourselves with assurances such as: *I'm doing all right here, aren't I? So many people are here, including most of my friends and family. It's feeling more like home every day. So, what's the point in climbing higher?* However, when the natural next step seems to be to take no step at all—just lose ourselves in the crowd and hope for the best—we're actually inviting trouble.

I want to propose a different course of action: *do what you came to do and don't let fear throw you off.* My wife, Cindy, and I love to hike and climb in the mountains. Best of all is when our sons are with us and it's a Team Reeter adventure. Whether it's a fourteener or an easy ascent to a beautiful vista or waterfall, I've noticed that before we start, there's always a little anxiety. Especially on the tougher climbs. If we're not careful, we could easily talk ourselves out of going at all. It never fails, though: once we set out on our adventure, we end up having so much fun, and enjoying such incredible sights, that it's hard to remember why we were anxious in the first place.

Leaving the comfort of base camp in our lives is similar. The first steps away from the trailhead are often the hardest, at least in our minds. However, nearly everyone feels that way. Instead of getting caught up in your anxiety, congratulate yourself that you made the decision to get off the couch and shoot for something better. Then remind yourself: "I came here to climb a mountain," take a deep breath, and…go! Before you know it, you'll be thanking yourself and planning your next adventure.

Not Everybody Stays

At different times in life, no matter how accomplished they are, everyone ends up in survival mode. But not everyone leads themselves beyond it. To me, this is the real tragedy of this level—that so few ever see even one summit in their time on earth. They never go after that "Mission accomplished!" moment that makes the effort of the trek worthwhile.

It is true that the beginning of every journey is where the most uncertainty exists. No one can predict everything that lies ahead. Yet that doesn't stop people from taking trips to amazing destinations around the world every day, and it shouldn't prevent you from setting out toward the amazing goals you carry within your heart.

If you *are* existing at survival level anywhere in your life, you do not have to stay there! Survival is not supposed to be a settling ground. Rather, it can and should be a starting point. By taking one intentional step after another, you can lead yourself out of survival and away from the crowd, to the next level and the next, and begin to change your life.

Life's avalanches do sometimes push people back down to base camp through no fault of their own. People who are thoroughly leading themselves in one arena, such as their marriage, can end up in survival conditions somewhere else, such as their job, because of circumstances beyond their control or because of others' poor choices. The difference is, they don't stay long enough to acclimate. (That's necessary for summiting Everest, not for excelling in your life.) They don't make this level their home away from home, and, therefore, it doesn't become their permanent "mode."

If you're living by default in any regard—having resigned yourself to the minimum existence (or sometimes the minimum effort) as a parent, an employee, a lover, a citizen; if you're hiding away in the crowd, content to be average—you're in the dangerous realm of survival in that particular area. And the longer you stick around, the more prone you are to claim its motto: "It is what it is; I just need to live with it."

Given enough time, that is exactly what everyone who opts to stay at survival level will teach themselves to do: *live with it*. And each time they do, they put more distance between themselves and the life they could have had.

I'm urging you to pack up your tent and strive higher because the clock is ticking, and the passage of time only increases the distance between you and your destiny. First of all, mountains continue to grow taller, both literally and in our mind's eye, the longer we wait. (Check out Quora.com and ScienceDaily.com for data on the annual growth of mountains like Everest and the rest of the Himalayas.) Second, to loosely paraphrase Newton's law of inertia, an object at rest tends to stay at rest and an object in motion tends to stay in motion. Things in a sedentary state deteriorate—our bodies, our relationships, and our skills. Opportunities evaporate when they're not acted on. Finally, as with the mountains of earth, there are only certain seasons in which we have a realistic chance at summiting. Experts call them "climbing windows." Failing to seize the day to lead ourselves upward and out of survival can, at some point, mean not only missing the goal but also the journey.

IS IT ALL JUST HAPPENING TO YOU?

Lots of people temporarily choose survival, especially when they're embarking on a new or bigger adventure. This makes sense when you're a rookie who needs to learn the ropes, or when you're sacrificing for the sake of a greater cause. Many of us early in our careers subsisted on cereal or peanut butter sandwiches to ensure that we could cover rent. Or we rode a bike or a bus to work until we could afford a car. Others have given up their social life or family time for a while in order to return to school and earn their college degree. But those who opt to stay at the bottom of their mountain challenge indefinitely are most susceptible to letting fear stamp out what could have been.

Rather than attempting to reach the utmost level in their marriages, careers, or personal fitness, many travelers on life's journey have retreated from the pursuit, lowered their expectations, and settled in for the long haul. Settled for having a job versus a career. A spouse rather than a best friend and partner. A religion rather than a relationship with God in faith.

Here are some markers for determining if you're not just temporarily in survival mode but actually living in permanent survival mode. Mark any that are true for you, and use these to determine which areas to address so that you can soon be on your way.

Are you...

- o   eating poorly, skipping exercise, and expecting your body to somehow stay healthy?
- o   leaving your money unmanaged (or maybe in the hands of your creditors)?
- o   allowing your friendships to reside at surface level?
- o   living beyond your means and then hoping for rescue?
- o   letting your job take you where it will?
- o   coasting in your family relationships?
- o   looking for an "out" without caring about the outcome (where it leads)?
- o   finding comfort in the crowd?
- o   so paralyzed at the prospect of failure that you won't even try?

If you...

- o lose your job, will your future be in jeopardy?
- o lose that significant someone, will you be permanently lost?
- o lose your title or position, will you consider yourself a no-body?

Have you...

- o surrendered your desires to follow the crowd?
- o decided that somebody else needs to fix what's wrong in your world?
- o believed the lie that big dreams are for other people?

THE NEXT LEVEL:
FROM SURVIVAL TO SUCCESS

In the lead-yourself journey, the level immediately beyond survival is *success*. You've not yet reached the summit, but you've made it further than most. There's nothing wrong with success. Who doesn't want the adventure, the sense of accomplishment, the accolades that come with this territory? It's a blessing that opens up opportunities and connections that aren't available when you're in survival mode. And there's no denying, it can be a really fun place to hang out.

In my view, though, success includes more than this. It means you've progressed from uncomfortable to more comfortable. Seeking comfort and maintaining comfort is overrated, though. Life is meant to be an uncomfortable adventure of growth. At our firm we often say, "We are seeking to become comfortable being uncomfortable."

Applied to life, people who reach this level are not only (hopefully) accumulating expertise and financial security but, more importantly, growing in wisdom and character and gaining greater favor with God and with others. Besides being intent on building a better life for both themselves and their loved ones, they are ideally discovering an increasing sense of joy and purpose in who they are and what they do.

A Subtle Danger

A particularly subtle danger exists at this middle level, and we must guard hard against it. The danger is comfort—growing content and setting down roots, perhaps perceiving that you've reached your goal and gone high enough, when, in reality, the top of the mountain is still a ways off.

The temptation is understandable. Unless you're one of those freakishly gifted climbers for whom success has come naturally, you're probably pretty tired from the sacrifice, time, and training involved with getting here. So, why not stay put? A life of success is a nice life. It's a far less populated "territory" than survival, which means there's room for everybody to spread out. Plus, it usually comes with a spouse, a car, a house, a couple of kids, a cool job title, prestige, a fat 401(k)…and bragging rights: "I've made it further than anybody else I know, including my parents, the people I went to school with, and everybody I work with."

There was a time in my younger days when I thought success as society defines it—achieving a big name, a big title, a big bank account, and/or a big following—was the highest outcome anyone could hope for. I've since learned that "the name and the fame" (and everything that comes with them) are perks along the way, but not the peaks of anyone's life pursuit. They're hilltops on your path to increasingly higher summits, but not the true, plant-your-flag conquests you're destined for.

The more I was given access beyond the surface of people's lives, the more apparent this became. Many of my clients were succeeding in certain areas (often their work and financial life) but barely surviving in the most important things, such as their marriage. Or they'd proven successful in some ways, but they also admitted to feeling unfulfilled otherwise, even disappointed or disillusioned. Emotionally speaking, while they were not terribly unhappy at this level, they weren't as happy as they could be, or wanted to be.

This told me two things: First, that success in some categories doesn't mean you're leading yourself in all areas. Second, while the rewards of success are nice, they can quickly distract and divert us from the real prize.

Success simply is not the apex of our existence on this earth. If it were, our celebrity heroes who can afford every material possession would stop confessing feelings of deep emptiness in their memoirs— and stop manifesting it in their lives. There would be fewer headliners in sports, entertainment, and business plummeting into addiction, multiple divorces, estrangement from their kids, crime, and even suicide. Nearly four out of five NFL players wouldn't be in financial peril within two years of retiring from the game, and three out of five NBA players wouldn't be bankrupt within five years of retirement.[3]

Based on what I observed, it was evident that there is yet another level to aspire to: we need to lead ourselves to *significance*, where we're not only passionately pursuing our full potential but *actively establishing and sustaining* the highest of outcomes—ones that permanently influence or change lives beyond our own for the better.

You may be tempted to stop just below the summit, but don't. If you stop at the level of success, where has your climbing gotten you? You've spent all these hours working to be somebody, to surpass somebody, to catch up to somebody, to be like somebody, or to *show them* (whomever that is from your past). But if you've given up on the peak and never seen those views…if you've quit exploring and expanding your horizons…if you're no longer challenging yourself to strive further…if you're doing things just for you and not out of love for others…then you're falling short of what you were made for. You haven't yet reached the rare air at the top where you are not only thriving at the highest levels of your purpose, but also encouraging and helping others to climb higher, too.

So, don't mistake success for the summit. Trust me, you want the summit!

THE SUMMIT OF SIGNIFICANCE

Ultimately, leading yourself means more than merely surviving or greatly succeeding; it means forging your own path toward your peak existence in the realms that are meaningful to you. The end goal is significance. Nothing less will do.

Lead yourself for a lifetime, in all the areas that matter to you, and you'll reach that peak many times over. What's more, you will begin to bring others with you; for significance is the place where you turn around, extend a rope toward someone else, and help them toward their dreams. Think of a life of significance as one that pursues eternal outcomes, not just the temporary attributes of success. Finishing well, not just starting strong.

The primary concern at this uppermost level is: What are you doing that's going to outlive you? What are you doing that others, especially your great-grandchildren (and even the great-grandchildren of your friends), will benefit from? I'm asking about actions well beyond creating wealth and leaving your loved ones financially secure. I'm also asking regardless of your age. Don't think for one second that leading yourself to significance is only for "old" people. Even if you are fresh out of college, what timeless truths and principles are you passing down? What kind of character are you exemplifying? How are you building toward a more enduring cause than just your own little kingdom? Which seeds are you planting that will bloom long after you're gone?

The difference between success and significance is that of planting one tree that you and your family can enjoy during your lifetime…and planting an entire orchard that will continue to feed and shade others long after you're gone. When you focus on significance throughout your life, you don't just yield a harvest in your own yard; the people around you take the seeds you've handed them and plant orchards of their own.

That kind of increase is at the heart of living by design at the highest level. Once you have reached significance, you stop living by default and start doing a different kind of math. Your focus turns from addition to multiplication. From gaining to giving. From paying back to paying things forward. From investing in "stuff" to leaving a generous deposit in people's hearts and lives.

Changing Priorities

My father, brother, and I grew up hunting together. We hunted just about every species of critter you can imagine, and I've had the good fortune of successful hunts since I was a young man.

While I'm not even the best hunter in my family (my father, when he was younger, could kill an in-flight quail with a .22, and my brother is one of the most skilled marksmen I know), I've always been enthusiastic about the sport. There was a time when no challenge was too large for me—I'd shoot an arrow at anything in pursuit of a venison steak or an elk tenderloin. In fact, there came a time not too many years ago when I had harvested so many elk that my wife declared, "Enough! Nothing else will fit on our walls." Me? I simply took this as a challenge to kill something larger than what we already had on display, in order to replace a smaller trophy mount.

Over the years, though, I've seen my sporting objectives change, and it reflects a change in how I lead myself in life, too. I'm a lot less concerned these days with the success of my hunts and more focused on the meaning behind the experience. For example, I'm intent on creating big memories with my buddies or my sons versus focusing on the size of an animal. And I love to sit and commune with my Maker, inspired by the beauty of His handiwork, making notes in my Life Book while envisioning the future. A Life Book is a leather-bound book that I do life in. It's more than a journal, with tabs and sections for living more intentionally.

My pursuit is less for the majestic *wapiti* (the Shawnee and Cree term for elk), or white-tailed deer, than for a greater fulfillment of my various callings and life purpose. Just last season at our ranch, a beautiful fourteen-point buck was twenty-five yards from the tip of my archery arrow. I chose not to shoot because I wanted my brother, who is fighting cancer, or one of my sons to have the joy of that harvest.

Don't get me wrong. I still love to hunt. I particularly love to hunt, spot, and stalk animals up in the mountains. But it's no longer my primary reason for the pursuit.

As you begin to pursue significance rather than success, you'll see the same sort of change in your priorities. Whereas you once cared primarily about your income, you'll care more about your impact. Instead of obsessing over business or real estate acquisitions, you'll be more concerned with acquiring lifelong friends. Rather than focusing so much on stocks and bonds, you'll look to invest in the people who are following in your footsteps.

Move in One Direction

On our journey through life, we will ideally progress from survival to success to significance in each of the areas we consider to be a priority: vocation, family, marriage, fitness, faith, and so on. The route is rarely smooth or continuous from one level to the next—life just isn't that predictable. Sometimes we will find ourselves thriving in a few areas and barely surviving in others. And even if we're operating at the height of significance in particular roles, and successfully making our way higher elsewhere, we can be sent backward without warning by a layoff, illness, or injury. Still, by leading ourselves, we can handle the future effectively, no matter what setbacks we encounter.

As you lead yourself, you'll be forging your path out of a mundane existence and toward a wildly meaningful one, hopefully all the way to the height of your potential. I'm not suggesting this comes easily, without a lot of work, but the objective is not hard to understand. In essence, throughout this entire journey, as you explore and define your individual path, you want to keep heading in one direction and one direction only: up.

Life sometimes sends you down. You might temporarily rabbit-trail to one side of the mountain or the other. But you will discover your best life by literally stepping *up* into something new.

Today's your day. The climbing window is open. Go forth and conquer.

CHAPTER 4

YOUR PEAK EXISTENCE

One experience in the fall of 2011 solidified for me the importance of continuing to lead myself as high as I can for as long as I can. That October, I turned fifty. In case this milestone is still ahead of you, let me tell you: a fiftieth birthday can be cause for a lot of reflection. I did plenty of looking back over my life in 2011, but I was also excited to keep pushing toward new goals and dreams. As part of my process, I embarked that January on a yearlong personal project (I called it "2020 Vision"), in which I sought to define how I wanted my future to unfold. I thought through all the life events that were likely to occur between that landmark year and the year 2020, as well as my relationships and dreams, and I asked myself: *How can I prepare now to be equal to those challenges? What am I being called to do in order to* *make the most of those experiences and opportunities?* I visualized maximizing our financial-services firm, not only for profitability but for the ultimate goal: impact in the lives of our clients, our advisers, and our teams. I looked ahead to an even greater future with Cindy as my best friend and partner. I thought about our grown sons and how I could better mentor each of them. I envisioned daughters-in-law and grandchildren, and I reinforced the importance of staying physically fit so I could be around to enjoy them. And I reflected on my love for America and ways I could be an even more proactive citizen. It was a wonderful, future-forward exercise.

As my birthday drew closer, I began to hear the mountains calling my name. Having always believed that the One who stirs the wind also walks the high places of the earth, I felt that the mountains would be the perfect setting to spend time with my Creator at the midcentury mark in my journey.

In my mind, such a milestone birthday called for an awesome outing—and to me, that meant heading out on a hunt with some of my "warrior brothers." So, I decided on a bowhunting trip for elk in the splendor and majesty of the Colorado Rockies, and I invited three of my best buddies to join me: Stephen Barnes, Bob Reccord, and Joe White. I couldn't think of a better way to get fired up for the next fifty years of impact (God willing).

Thankfully, I know Al Snyder of the Fish and Cross Ranch in northwest Colorado. A seasoned outfitter, Al and his family own and run this hunting ranch—twenty thousand acres in the Routt National Forest—as part of a profound leadership vision. They have also established a wonderful program for people who need to find some renewal.

Al graciously reserved our group a week on their calendar, and on September 18, the guys and I departed our respective homes in Texas, Missouri, and Washington, DC, for an epic time of fellowship in the great outdoors. Upon our arrival in Colorado, the four of us were literally giddy. What an awesome opportunity to get away from the pressurized situations that were pulling at each of us and be boys for a while.

Al had hand-selected some of the most talented hunting guides in that region: Trey, who was assigned to Stephen and Bob; and Ethan for Joe and me. Our hunting trip entailed hiking many miles up and down hills each day with heavy packs on our backs, carrying bows, arrows, and other equipment. Each morning, just after 4:00 a.m., we would get up, pack our gear, and take a truck as far as the terrain would allow, bouncing and careening along the mountain ridges until we reached a spot where we would have to hike on foot. Sometimes at around 11:00 a.m. we would head back down to the lodge for lunch and what was supposed to be a nap, though the need for sleep was usually forgotten amid our heart-to-heart conversations. Around 3:30 p.m., we would head back to the mountains.

The evening hunts were the most powerful. We would hike and stalk, hike and call until about ninety minutes before sundown. Then our guides would situate us in an area that they believed had great potential, and we would set up for some prime hunting, all the while experiencing the Rockies' stunning sunsets.

One of those evenings, I was with Joe and Ethan at just over ten thousand feet, in an area nicknamed Boogie Bear Park where several game trails converge into one. Between the evidence of a lot of animal activity and the fact that we had seen a bull elk and a cow elk pass by on a previous hunt, Joe and I were excited about the opportunity before us. Joe set up in a hidden area overlooking the convergence point. Ethan positioned himself about thirty yards away to do the calling and spotting. He primarily did cow calls, emulating the sound of a female elk, but occasionally he would do a bugle call, which is both majestic and wonderful, especially when a bull elk bugles back. For a bowhunter in September, that is about as good as it gets.

I set up my spot approximately seventy yards from Ethan and probably eighty yards from Joe, in a fantastic position behind a couple of large logs. Those logs overlooked a spread of aspen trees and gave me a clear view of any elk that might wander down the mountain for the evening in the direction of the meadows. Having created great cover for myself, I was really optimistic about this spot.

Once situated in my hunting area, I stayed mostly on my knees. Hunting on my knees helps me keep my head low, reducing the chance that the wildlife will see me. It was also the appropriate posture for this specific trip. In that time on my knees, I thought again about my future. I journaled in my Life Book for courage and strength, and renewed my commitment to a high calling, a high standard, for the remainder of my days, literally writing: "Although I don't know how much time I have left, I want to be all in."

I had no idea how timely those words would soon be.

As dusk descended, I heard a loud noise behind me, coming through the trees in my direction. Hoping it might be a large bull elk with a monstrous rack of antlers, I carefully turned and set up in the opposite direction in order to have a full view of where I anticipated the animal would emerge. I readied myself, my bow on full draw, as the noise traveled behind some bushes about twenty-five yards out and then moved away from me at a cross angle.

In that instant, the source of the noise came into view, and it was no elk! It was a large, adult black bear traveling on all fours, and he was close—within a matter of yards! Stupidly, I turned my back on him and walked a few steps to place my bow on a peg. That's when the bear started coming right at me! I drew my sidearm, a 9mm Ruger pistol, and held my position as best I could, but he was closing in so quickly that I remember almost nothing except the adrenaline rush.

Suddenly, upon reaching a fallen aspen log that was about eight yards in front of me, this massive beast stopped abruptly, stood on his back legs, and hissed. Then the hiss rolled into a growl that bellowed through Boogie Bear Park. Within milliseconds, I debated my options: I could propel myself backward through my blind in order to buy time. Or I could shoot, aiming either for the heart or the face (though my pistol was little better than a pellet gun, and honestly, I was shaking so hard that I wasn't sure I'd even graze him). Instead, I was providentially led to step toward the bear with intensity.

Apparently, I surprised him, because he turned his head, still looking at me…and then backed down to all fours and took cover to his left amid some trees and bushes. I followed his movement with my gun, my hands and arms still quivering. A few moments later, he again rose up on his hind legs, hissed, and then growled so loudly that I felt like I was being stalked by *him*! Then, as quickly as he'd risen up, the bear moved back to all fours and stepped into an open space to his left. Looking right at me, he hissed once more before jogging back into the woods.

Ethan later told me, "I've been hunting this area for eighteen years, and that was one of the largest bears I've ever seen!"

LIFE LESSONS

Reflecting on this intense memory, I am thankful to have walked away from that incident with my future intact. It was certainly a reminder that my next breath is not a given and that we never know what we're going to encounter. Putting that in perspective is sobering. On the one hand, it makes me profoundly aware that I am not in control and that life is short. On the other hand, knowing that my days are numbered stokes my internal fires and makes me want to maximize every experience.

The average adult's "climbing window" for life on this earth, assuming he or she stays healthy, amounts to roughly twenty-one thousand days. I don't know about you, but to me, that doesn't sound like a lot of time. And the older I get, the faster those days fly. For as long as I live, I must keep leading myself forward, making each stride count. Whether I'm working to achieve my goals or spending time with my family or making decisions on behalf of my team at work, my choices matter, both now and for the future. They can mean life or death to my own hopes and dreams and the hopes and dreams of the people I care about.

Here's something else I gleaned from my fearfully incredible encounter with a creature so much bigger than myself: it reinforced for me that if I want those once-in-a-lifetime experiences, I dare not back down. I have to "step up my game" and go for my goals even when an obstacle is standing in my way. In this instance, it may literally have saved my life.

I can see now how the years of leading myself prepared me for that moment. The years of training and practice and guided hunts kicked in for sure. But the fact that I instinctively stepped toward the challenge instead of away from it *in spite of my fear* encourages me to this day. When forced to make a choice, I chose to act. To play offense. To step forward with all the intensity I could muster, even though I was afraid.

Really, that's the first step toward significance for any of us. And it may be the most critical one of all. No great adventure happens without it.

WHAT LEADING YOURSELF LEADS TO

You've probably heard the old joke referred to by the characters in the movie *Everest*: Why did the man climb the mountain? Because it's there.

I'm not just urging you to shoot for all the summits you can because they're there. That may be reason enough for the most daring among us, but the rest of us (the majority of us) need more than bragging rights and a selfie at the peak. We need a greater purpose. And a greater reward.

Significance offers both.

A Greater Purpose

One conversation stands out to me in my journey toward choosing a greater purpose for leading myself. It was a chilly autumn night in November 1996. I was walking my five-year-old to our car at a country club in Denton, Texas, after my friend and colleague Kraig Stockdale's rehearsal dinner. Kraig had joined our Northwestern Mutual team in 1992, and I'd had the tremendous honor of being his field director. He'd become an extended member of the Reeter family almost instantly. Now he was marrying his sweetheart, Carrie, and my eldest son and I were in the wedding.

As I was getting my little boy in the car, I heard somebody say, "Hey Jeff, wait just a minute!" It was Kraig's dad, Ken. He had graciously hosted the dinner we'd just enjoyed in that wonderful setting. Throughout the evening, there had been toasts and jokes, well-wishes and sentimental reflections—and they all involved one common theme: Kraig and Carrie were principled young people with a really bright future, whose parents had raised them well. That's why Mr. Stockdale's words to come caught me by surprise.

"Thank you for the years you've spent mentoring and coaching Kraig," he said. "This is one of the greatest nights of my life." Then, Mr. Stockdale got emotional. "Kathy and I have been praying for you and Kraig for over twenty-six years."

Confused by his comment, I remarked, "Sir, I've only known Kraig for a little over four years."

"True, I wasn't praying for you by name, Jeff," he replied, "but twenty-six years ago I was praying for you as Kraig's first boss."

That moment is riveted in my mind. It felt providential. It felt important. It felt like what I was doing in my vocation was markedly more important than just helping men and women earn a living—I was helping them craft a life. Even more, I understood in that moment that when you lead yourself, not only will your life produce excellence, but it will *reproduce*.

As a result of that parking lot conversation with Kraig's dad, I began to think more intentionally about my own sons: *Who will be their first boss? Whom will they marry? What will they achieve? What will they contribute?* From that night till now, more than twenty years later, I've had those thoughts as key areas of vision casting, discussion, and prayer for all three of my boys.

Which brings me back to the foreword of this book. What my buddy Jeff Turner didn't tell you was that the young man sitting in front of him in the interview that day was Cindy's and my oldest son, Chad. Providentially, Chad's first boss is Jeff Turner. The man I had been mentoring since before Chad was born became the man I was praying for as Chad was growing up!

This is what leading yourself leads to. You enjoy not just an extraordinary life pursuit of your own, but some mountaintop moments where you have the chance to turn around and help others make their climb. It's a triple blessing: You don't just get the adventure today and make an impact now; your impact lives on in the people who knew you. And as they learn to lead themselves to significance, they will pass the know-how and the climbing ropes to other travelers, as Jeff Turner did with my son, and as I trust Chad will do with others one day. It reminds me of words from one of the great kings in history: the ones who focus on significance are "like a tree planted by streams of water, which yields its fruit in season and whose leaf does not wither—whatever they do prospers."[1]

When you're leading yourself at your peak level of existence, your labors are never in vain. Your efforts prosper while you live, allowing you to enjoy successes you wouldn't have had otherwise. Your efforts also bear fruit long after you're gone—in the lives of individuals you know…and in generations of individuals you'll never meet. This is one of the true indicators of a life of significance: your influence endures after you, particularly in people's minds and hearts. Your encouragement and example not only further their lives and thinking but can move them to uniquely impact "their" people, their world, for the better, inspiring *their* beneficiaries to strive further and higher, too.

Those lead-yourselfers who come behind you may exceed what you were ever able to do. If so, be excited and grateful, for isn't that why you're here? To make your mark while you can, on as many lives as you can?

Any time later generations reap from what you have so thoughtfully sowed, you are living out the purpose of significance. It's a reason that keeps on giving and giving, says one author: "When we use our time, talents, gifts, skills, and interests to serve others, God has a way of multiplying the impact and influence of these things many times over."[2]

A Greater Reward

There are so many rewards for pursuing significance, but one of my favorites is that it means you have staying power. I don't know anybody who doesn't want that.

Significance produces staying power in multiple ways. As you work your way up from survival and learn to navigate the unique challenges of your journey, you gain resilience and expertise. You achieve success, and success produces confidence and self-esteem. The higher you go, the more you learn about yourself as well: about what, and who, is important to you and why. This is the fuel that sustains your inner fire.

Once you've achieved your quest for significance in even one realm—gotten a glimpse of what you're truly capable of in living by your design at home, at work, or in your community—you gain another form of staying power: the ongoing desire to reach that level and stay there in every area of pursuit. And not only stay there but actually build there.

Climbers who reach the peak of Everest don't get to do either of those things. They have a few minutes to celebrate at the top, but then they must quickly turn back and head down the mountain to reach a lower camp before daylight—and their oxygen supply—runs out. By contrast, when you're living by design and leading yourself, you get to visit multiple summits as you fulfill your various callings and passions, and you can stay as long as you want.

Being able to stay and enjoy it is an ultimate reward. What's more, your friends and family get to join you for the experience. There's nothing like having your loved ones alongside you to celebrate and savor the views. Sharing any victory multiplies its joy. Finally, establishing yourself in significance means having a sacred privilege that few others have: the opportunity to build an enduring future for yourself and potentially for every person and cause you care about. *Staying power at its finest.*

At this peak level of existence, you're essentially laying a cornerstone atop every new summit. A cornerstone on which you can build not just a home but a homestead—the kind of magnificent, permanent place that will provide shelter and enjoyment for generations to come. To do so on a patch of prime real estate that no one's ever built on before is as exciting and meaningful and empowering as you'd expect. But at the end of every build, what really matters is that what you've done will last.

A life of significance is built on stone. Metaphorically speaking, when you build at the peak, you have an entire mountain beneath you! In exchange for the shifting ice of survival, you've gained an immovable foundation, reached a place where you can fix your purpose and identity, where they are no longer subject to the fickle winds of success.

There is a world of purpose and reward waiting precisely for you at this highest level if only you'll step toward the challenge rather than away from it. And every climber who's ever led themselves that far will tell you it's worth every risk and sacrifice required to reach it. Truthfully, the strength and permanence and fulfillment found in significance are so great that once you get there, you'll do more than celebrate. You'll ask yourself, *Why didn't I do this sooner?*

PART TWO

YOUR GLOBAL POSITION

CHAPTER 5

YOUR JOURNEY TILL NOW

Everybody gets a little lost or stuck sometimes—it comes with the territory of being human.

Not everyone, though, finds their way out. Starting with this section of the book, I want to help you not only find your way to success but guide you to go further and higher than perhaps you've ever thought possible.

One reason I'm so excited about showing you how to lead yourself is that there's no magic involved; anyone can do it. You'll have to choose to *step up* to the next level on your journey and *step toward* your challenges rather than away from them, as we've discussed. You'll also need to take a little inventory—answering some basic questions regarding who you are, where you are, and what you want. Using these questions, you'll develop a MAP (a Master Action Plan) that fits your design. And with this MAP in hand, you'll be ready to let your greatest adventures begin!

Not everyone wants to bother with taking inventory. Like me, you probably can name people you know who would prefer to live in denial about their present, their past, or even where their current path is taking them. Yet the truth is what really sets us free. So, for the sake of attaining an awesome future, commit that you will not back down from the questions in this chapter. Promise yourself that you will candidly assess the experiences you've had till now—and grab a legal pad to help you do it. You won't regret it. The advance toward your dreams begins in earnest once you're willing to accurately gauge where you are, and why.

WHERE ARE YOU?

For starters, let's find your blinking blue dot on the GPS of life.

This process deserves more than a glance. We're used to only peeking at our GPS as we travel, but when it comes to getting a read on your current location in life, quiet reflection and introspection are needed. Once you've scheduled a little time for some personal exploration, evaluate: *Where are you right now, in this season?* Go beyond the facts of where you live and work, or your relationship status; beyond how many kids you have or the cash in your checking account. I want you to dig deeper, assessing the truth regarding your position in each of five key areas: relationally, professionally, financially, physically, and spiritually. Answer each of the questions below, one area at a time.

Relationally…

- Are you living by default or design?
- On a scale of one to ten, to what degree are you living by default or design?
- At what level are you: survival, success, or significance?
- Are you stuck in any way, or are you actively progressing from one level to the next?

Once you've answered this group of questions for this category, move on to the other categories—professionally, financially, physically, spiritually—and, one by one, survey where you stand.

Next, consider: *How do you perceive your position in each of the five areas?* What's your mind-set about where you are relationally? Professionally? Financially? Physically? Spiritually?

Let's say you rated your physical health at a three and categorized yourself at survival level. You aren't on any medications, and you gave up sodas and sugary beverages a few months ago, but you still eat a fair amount of junk food, you're twenty pounds overweight, and you don't exercise. Do you view yourself as being *at the bottom* of your climb, or as *just beginning* your journey toward fitness?

Or maybe you're diligently living a healthy lifestyle and you assessed yourself at an eight. You abide by a doctor-recommended nutrition plan, your medical numbers (blood pressure, heart rate, cholesterol, BMI, etc.) are on point for someone your age, and you alternate between strength and cardio workouts four times a week. You're clearly succeeding in this area of your life. What's your mind-set about being at this level? Are you thinking, *I'm in better shape than anyone else my age—I'm good*, or do you have your sights set on pushing higher, such as maybe training for a 10K?

Next, consider: *How do you feel about your current position in each key area?* What key words and statements would you use to pinpoint your emotions? Do words like *disappointed, frustrated, afraid, weary,* and *lost* come to mind, or perhaps *content, encouraged, optimistic,* and *inspired*?

Finally, *what do your collective answers say about you?* Is your perception relatively upbeat or mostly negative? Does your mind-set suggest that you're open and teachable or stubborn and closed off? Do your word choices indicate that you have good momentum or that you've hit a wall, or possibly given up altogether?

If indications are that you're already leading yourself, then keep it going, and let's build on that progress! If you see evidence that you're living by default (and maybe didn't even know it), stick with me; that is all going to change starting with this chapter.

WHERE HAVE YOU BEEN?

Once you've done the exercises above, once you've claimed a patch of earth and said, "This is where I am," it's time to look back over your shoulder and assess: *How did I get to this spot? Who and what led me here?* This is important because your past, good and bad, is the foundation from which your future or destiny is launched.

Ask yourself: *How far am I from where I started out in life? What have I done with both the circumstances I've been given and the choices that were before me?* Also, consider the ways you've allowed the generational legacies you've inherited and the cultural messages you've embraced to affect your choices and mind-set, for better or for worse. Relationally, professionally, financially, physically, spiritually...

- Whose footsteps have you followed in, consciously or subconsciously?
- What spoken and unspoken rules have you lived by that you learned growing up?
- Which lies have kept you from creating a new legacy and which truths have you built on?
- What trends have distracted you from your destiny?

Reviewing the patterns of your past, as well as the messages you've integrated, will give you a fuller picture of how much you've lived by default and how much you've lived by design.

Next, explore this: *How well have those choices worked for me?* Evaluating whether you've exceeded your own expectations or fallen short of how far you hoped to be by now will help you determine what you'd like to do differently going forward.

YOUR DREAM STATE

Your answers to both inventories—about your current location and the places you've been—reveal *the state of your dreams*. To live by design, you must turn things around and decide: What is *my dream state*? In other words, what do you *really* want, not just for your life but for your relationships and your legacy? What do you want to say with your days? Leave for your children and grandchildren? Change for the better in your neighborhood and the world at large?

I'm convinced that we get what we want. You may be unwilling to admit it, or scared to commit, but you *will* get what you want. The question is, what *do* you want? I should qualify this a bit. It's not like a genie in a bottle, where you get your one wish. Truly, though, I have seen many examples of a diligent person setting a principled goal on a timetable and achieving that goal. Often that goal was initially deemed unlikely, maybe even impossible. Yet it was accomplished.

The typical adult's goal is to be comfortable and have certainty. Unfortunately, people give up a lot of great things for the cause of staying safe. In the pursuit of uncommon adventures, the goal has to be to "get comfortable with being uncomfortable." This is what makes a leader. Living on purpose, by design, doesn't necessarily give you safety; sometimes it drives you deeper into unknown territory, at least initially. But as you venture into those new frontiers, you'll find you've been drawn higher, where dreams are made.

Much of America turned on their black-and-white television sets with "rabbit ear" antennas in September 1962 to hear President John F. Kennedy present a vision of what was possible on a previously unexplored frontier. And an entire nation bought into that dream of space conquest:

> Why, some say, the moon? Why choose this as our goal? And they may well ask why climb the highest mountain? Why, thirty-five years ago, fly the Atlantic?…We choose to go to the moon. We choose to go to the moon in this decade, and do the other things, not because they are easy, but because they are hard; because that goal will serve to organize and measure the best of our energies and skills; because that challenge is one that we are willing to accept, one we are unwilling to postpone, and one which we intend to win.[1]

He put the desire into words, and in less than a decade, this crazy, completely "out there" idea had been realized.

Kennedy knew that if you shoot for the moon (or in our context, the stratosphere of significance), you're far more likely to reach it. If you keep climbing higher, special things happen. Yes, you'll have to plan carefully and draw from deep inside yourself to make the push past your comfort zone. Any worthwhile pursuit will test your energies, your skills, your fortitude. Yet that's how you end up in some pretty remarkable places.

PERSPECTIVE: A DECIDING FACTOR

Your life experience may have turned up more adversity than accomplishment in your past. Or this may be true of your present situation. Nonetheless, your perspective is a deciding factor in your journey.

My mom was a professional psychologist, and she often talked about a phenomenon that she saw play out over and over in her clients' lives. Her patients came from every type of background—abused, abandoned, affluent, impoverished, addicted, neglected, coddled. Surprisingly, what they had *actually* experienced didn't predict their future successes or failures nearly as much as how they viewed their experiences. What my mom saw firsthand was the link between hindsight and foresight: how dramatically and directly her clients' beliefs about the legacies they'd inherited affected their destiny. Some of them viewed their difficulties as dead ends; others understood their experiences as adding to their lives rather than subtracting from them. The ones who found healing took on the attitude that "when life leaves its mark on you, you have the opportunity to leave your mark on it."

Ben Carson is a prime example. Ben's mom had only a third-grade education, and his father left the family for good when Ben was only eight, sinking the family into poverty. All through grade school in Detroit, Ben was considered the class dummy by his peers. But his devoted mom believed in hard work, no excuses, and doing your best—and she was convinced that Ben was destined for more. She pushed both of her boys to quit watching TV and start reading, and in time, Ben discovered a love of learning and a proficiency for science.

One day at church, Ben realized that he wanted to be a doctor. His mom told him many times growing up: "If you let others' actions and words determine what you do, there's no real point in having a mind of your own. Use that brain God gave you…to make your own decisions, to choose your own path. Don't let [anyone] rob you of that choice."[2]

In high school, Ben took those words to heart. The classes in his inner-city school were frequently disrupted by troublemakers, but Ben decided that going along with the mayhem was not for him. Neither was giving in to the defeatist mind-set that often hid behind such behavior. Intent on obtaining an education, he actively sought out his teachers after class in order to ask further questions and dig deeper into the subject matter.[3]

Through college at Yale and then at medical school back in Michigan, Carson led himself to success, becoming the chief of pediatric neurosurgery at Johns Hopkins Hospital at the age of thirty-three (the youngest major division director in the hospital's history), and then to significance as a pioneering surgeon. After conquering such odds, no one could have blamed him if he'd spent the rest of his life in medicine. Still, he believed he could do more. His extraordinary speech at the National Prayer Breakfast in 2013 changed the trajectory of a nation, instilling the idea that a nonpolitician could be president. He courageously entered the campaign for president of the United States prior to the 2016 election. And though he did not ultimately win the candidacy for the White House, he works tirelessly as the secretary of housing and urban development in the current administration.

Pastor Charles Swindoll has written that "life is 10 percent what happens to us and 90 percent how we respond to it."[4] And so it is with you. We are in charge of our attitudes. Ben Carson grew up in a survival situation, but as soon as he was old enough to realize he could lead himself, he took the perspective that nothing was going to hold him down: not the hardship of his past nor the difficulty of his present. Changing his perspective changed his belief about his possibilities. And once he changed his belief, he took steps to change his life.

To lead yourself means that adversity and misfortune need never be perceived as limitations. To the contrary, they are opportunities to start moving ahead in ways you never have before, and for reasons you never have before. Instead of, "Nothing good can come out of this!" which is the cry of people who live by default, we come to see that "my best—and my entire future—is coming out of this!" Others may view the situations you've been through, right down to your current trials and tests, as handicaps. With the right perspective, however, your present and your past can become stepping-stones to the kind of future you've always wanted.

Resilience enables us to thrive, according to Jamais Cascio. That is its goal. "Ultimately, resilience emphasizes increasing our ability to withstand crises," he writes. "It's all about being able to overcome the unexpected."[5]

How does all of this work together? An overcoming, lead-yourself attitude produces endurance. Endurance produces perseverance. Perseverance produces character. Character produces hope. And hope never, ever disappoints us.

In other words, trials are just as capable of tipping your scales toward success and significance as toward survival. It's all in your attitude, explains Swindoll:

> Words can never adequately convey the incredible impact of our attitude toward life...I believe the single most important decision I can make on a day-to-day basis is my choice of attitude. It is more important than my past, my education, my bankroll, my successes or failures, fame or pain, what other people think of me or say about me, my circumstances, or my position. Attitude...keeps me going or cripples my progress. It alone fuels my fire or assaults my hope. When my attitude is right, there's no barrier too high, no valley too deep, no dream too extreme, no challenge too great for me.[6]

That is a powerful quote. Things will happen to us. Things have happened to us. Your perspective, your attitude, plays a significant role regardless of where you are and where you've been. It's what propels you to keep leading yourself during survival times, successful times, and times of significance.

Identify how you have been changed for the better because of your trials and tests, and use those truths as logs for your fire. Then let that fire light your way as you climb. Are you propelling forward in a powerful way, or sitting idly in the ashes of your upbringing? You not only can lead yourself out of the ashes and beyond the legacy you've been given, but you must. Affirm what is true about your journey thus far, turn it for the positive, and then use that as your starting block toward a future that can't be denied.

THE POWER OF WHAT WILL BE

People who live by default will tell you that our futures are fixed, that the legacies we inherit dictate the destinies ahead of us. Absolutely not. You can't change your past, but you can change its effect on everything that you experience from now on. *You* choose the trajectory of your life. *You* determine the way forward. No matter your story so far, *you* decide the outcome.

It's a choice with far-reaching implications. My mom helped her clients to look truthfully at their lives and realize: *these things have brought me to this moment in time, but I get to choose my destiny from this day forward.* Thankfully, your life has much more to it than what was, or even what is. Maybe some of your dreams were delayed by others' choices or put on hold by adverse circumstances. The great thing about leading yourself is that you can choose not to postpone them any longer. You can break out and choose extraordinary any day.

Now is not the final word for those who lead themselves. Neither is *what was.*

What will be is what matters most.

Remember: "Default" doesn't define you unless you let it. You may be temporarily lost, a little stuck, or moving slower than you'd like, but you're not doomed to this as your destiny. You can live by your design and choose a new legacy, a different future, any day. Why not today?

Legendary basketball coach John Wooden said, "Yesterday's gone; we can do nothing about it. Tomorrow is yet to be. The only thing we can do to benefit tomorrow is what we do today." Regardless of your present or your past, it's never too late to blaze a new trail. As long as you have life and breath, you can create a future that is far different from the legacy you inherited, or even different from the one you've been pursuing.

Exhibit A: Alfred Nobel. In his lifetime, Alfred was best known as the inventor of dynamite. During a forty-five-year career as a highly successful chemist and engineer, he received a total of 355 patents for his inventions, but dynamite—which he developed in the quest for safer and more stable explosives than were being used in industry and armaments at the time—was the source of the majority of his wealth.

In 1888, one of Alfred's brothers died unexpectedly while on a trip to France. Some sources claim that, upon Ludvig's death, a French newspaper published Alfred's obituary instead, in a case of mistaken identity. Translated into English, the obituary's headline read: "The merchant of death is dead" and derided Alfred as one who "became rich by finding ways to kill more people faster than ever before." This glimpse of how he would be remembered if he continued on his current path was supposedly so upsetting that it prompted Alfred to rewrite his will and earmark nearly all of his massive fortune to establish and fund what he is known for more than a century after his death: the Nobel Prize, which annually honors individuals whose efforts have vastly benefited mankind in the sciences, literature, economics, and, most distinctively, the promotion of peace.

Truly, *any day* can be that day when we step away from what has been and lead ourselves toward a new tomorrow. Not sure how to get there, but you want a fresh start? The next chapter will help you set the course for what your tomorrows can look like and all the places they can take you.

CHAPTER 6

WHERE AM I GOING?

We all have times when we make less progress than others. In those times, having a longer-term vision of where we're headed can make a big difference. That age-old statement that without a vision, people perish, I believe, is truth. In addition, I believe that with a vision, people often thrive. To say that a different way, people who have a destination don't stay lost or stuck if they can help it.

Suppose you and your family are headed to Disney World from Pensacola, Florida. You've planned this vacation for months. You've saved up for it, talked about it, and even worked some overtime so you could be undistracted for the entire week. The kids are absolutely elated about this trip. What happens if, after passing through Tallahassee, you miss the I-75 South exit toward Orlando? Would you continue heading east and decide to spend the week in Jacksonville instead? Should you get a flat tire along the way, would you tell the kids, "We'll just sit this vacation out, right here on the shoulder of the road"? Of course not! You'd fix the tire, turn the car around, and, with the help of your GPS, backtrack until you found the road to Orlando.

This illustrates the value of having a vision. When you have a goal, a destination in your mind's eye, it focuses you as you travel. It motivates you to reroute should you get off course. Most importantly, it helps you know where you're going, quite literally multiplying your chances of completing your mission.

During my junior year in high school, my football team lost the biggest game of our lives—the state championship game. We were the Jenks Trojans, and this loss fed the legend that Jenks was jinxed and couldn't win the big one. My fellow juniors and I, however, had a different outcome—a different destination—in mind for our senior season, and we dedicated ourselves to it daily for the next year. Sure enough, it happened. Jenks High School won the Oklahoma state championship in 1979.

Since then, Jenks has seldom been defeated in championship games. The Trojans, since 1979, have won it all sixteen times and, during one stretch, took home the trophy six times in a row. The class of 1980 changed the trajectory of Jenks High School football, establishing a new and proud legend that its players live out to this day.

Roughly a year later, I found myself in the pregame locker room at Baylor, surrounded by my college teammates. Truly, I was just happy to be suited up. Baylor was ranked in the top twenty teams in the nation, but we had lost for the first time in the season just the week before, upset by San Jose State. On this Saturday afternoon, in front of a national television audience, we would be playing the Arkansas Razorbacks at home. Coach Grant Teaff, one of the most motivational people I have ever met, planned for our teammate and hero, Kyle Woods, to give the pregame speech. This was a monumental moment. Kyle had been tragically paralyzed the year before during a practice.

In the locker room that day, Kyle Woods stood for the first time since his injury. Then he looked at us, eyeing our entire team, and said, "You have to turn a setback into a comeback."

When Kyle said those words, I instantly realized: We have choices in life. We can make good things out of bad circumstances by setting our sights ahead of us. Kyle put that clearly in perspective.

IN THE RIGHT DIRECTION

If you know where to look, you'll know where to go. If you know where to look, your life will follow. Human anatomy demonstrates it perfectly. We each have a pair of eyes and a pair of feet pointing in the same direction: forward. Thus, we automatically steer toward what we see. Have you ever noticed that?

Think about the last time you were distracted by something along the side of the road while driving your car. Whether you were rubbernecking at a tow truck helping a disabled vehicle on the right shoulder, or you were curious about progress at the construction site to your left, you drifted in that direction for as long as you looked.

In every area of life, where you focus your attention is important. *The secret to moving—and especially living—in the right direction is to set your sights in the right direction.* This is Stage 1 of our Master Action Plan.

In the specific process of leading yourself, there are two ways to accomplish this:

1. You must envision worthy destinations—destinations that will exceed the effort it took to get there.

2. You must keep your eyes on the road ahead of you, not the world around you. I love the age-old statement about staying focused while running your race. It says that, because we each have a great cloud of witnesses watching, we should set aside anything that entangles us or slows us down and run the race with our eyes on the finish line.

WORTHY DESTINATIONS

My late father, Dale Victor Reeter, is one of my life heroes who taught me a lot about looking ahead and intentionally pursuing life by design. Being the systems guy that he was, he often stated that "failing to plan is planning to fail." In my mind, I can still hear him saying that. Growing up under his roof meant that envisioning and systematically planning for big things was a part of life. And one of the first things he taught me was: be fearless about developing a bold vision.

Go for the Bold

On the first afternoon of a week of training camp at our ranch, I ask our brand-new financial advisers to answer the question of this chapter ("Where are you going?") by drawing pictures on an oversize sheet of white paper—a storyboard—and then talking us through it. This adult art project has nothing to do with their artistic ability; I just want to get an idea of what's in their sights, how they're sizing up their future.

Very often, the visions that these outstanding men and women have are somewhat small. Or at least, smaller than they're capable of. This timidity at "going big" is something we have to get over, so let's give fearlessness a try, shall we? For the next few minutes, let's agree to go for the bold and practice visualizing bigger things. You can start with this: *What are your God-sized dreams for your marriage, your kids, your money, your friendships, your career, your community?*

Don't just envision what would be nice, fine, average, or ordinary; choosing a happy medium will not get you a mountaintop view. Visualize the best—and you at your best. See it in your mind. Think of what would energize you and bring you joy—what really makes your blood rush.

This is what I call the View of the Summit. It's a necessary starting point in your Master Action Plan because when we envision lofty goals, we make surer, stronger plans. With a bold vision leading the way, great things become possible.

Go Long

You also need to "go long" and cast your sights far enough out to find your finish. As we saw in the last chapter, where you are today has been greatly impacted by decisions you made five years ago. Likewise, five, ten, or fifty years from now, you will be where you are because of your decisions today, tomorrow, and all the days after that. So, do as leadership expert Stephen Covey recommends: "Begin with the end in mind."[1] Once you establish a longer-term vision, you can trace out the individual steps of your journey.

Author Mark Batterson explains: "The key to dreaming big is *thinking long*. And the bigger the dream, the longer the timeline." Therefore, if you're concerned with making an eternal impact, "you should have some dreams that can't be accomplished in your lifetime."[2] Finding the finish is exactly what gives dedicated mountain climbers the guts to willingly risk life and limb to stand atop a rugged peak. They don't just want a view *of* the summit; they long to see the view *from* the summit. And so, they lay claim to big, bold destinations somewhere in the distance and play it out in their minds.

They can see themselves cresting the mountain, shouting for joy at this monumental feat, and taking in the views from every direction. They can feel the elation of stepping foot onto the peak. They picture celebrating with the people they care about via satellite or even FaceTime, and then coming home to a circle of excited hugs and slaps on the back. And, if they're striving for significance, they imagine the fulfillment of using what they've learned to help other climbers experience the thrill, too. Who knows? Their own grandchildren or great-grandchildren may one day follow in their footsteps, confidently pursuing enormous dreams and making incredible memories—all because they went for it. Or perhaps some adventurers they have yet to meet will be inspired by their experiences and go after mountains of their own someday.

If it works for mountain climbers, it can work for the rest of us.

Where you are now—whether in survival or success—isn't going to suffice a few years down the road. So, the question is: Five years from today, where do you want to be in in your marriage? Your finances? Your health and fitness? If you could visualize yourself in a better or even extraordinary place, enjoying a more optimum experience, where would you be? The question is purposely five years out, not five months from now. This longer view takes the pressure off. (Incidentally, people usually reach these goals in three to four years if they're intentional.) What would your ideal be like? Stake out your dreams and then state them. Picture yourself living them in full color, and then own them by writing them down, in the present tense, as if they've already happened. I like to call that a "V60," which stands for "Victory in 60 months."

If you're married, don't be afraid to declare as your V60 goal: "My spouse and I are truly best friends." If you're single, avow a marriage where there is fidelity, camaraderie, laughter, lots of shared adventures, and great compatibility. With your health, visualize and verbalize your end goal: "I'm down to 180 pounds, have great biceps and six-pack abs, and I can run a mile in under seven minutes."

Go for Real, but with Optimism

Part three of this vision strategy is important to describe carefully. My favorite book on the planet says that we should exercise caution in boasting about tomorrow, because we can't guarantee what will happen. Thus, over the years, some of my colleagues and I have come up with the concept of Plan C.

I think everyone is familiar with the concept of Plan A, which refers to ideal circumstances and outcomes, and Plan B, which typically refers to the next-best alternative. The View of the Summit exercise is designed to help us arrive at our longer-term plan for one day. We visualize that plan based on the best versions of ourselves coming forward and creating great outcomes. It's Plan A, built on sheer optimism.

In addition to visualizing this plan with optimism, we must also focus on realism. It's very unlikely that everything will unfold seamlessly. What do you do then? In other life-planning systems, this is where Plan B would be recommended—not with a Master Action Plan, however. Because here's what I have learned: nobody wants to settle for Plan B. Instead, you develop a Plan C. Plan C puts the things that are out of our *Control* into *Context*. *Plan C says we are going to Courageously be Committed to Controlling what we Can Control and letting go of what we Can't Control with Contentment.*

Plan A allows you to envision the very best and do your very best, while Plan C empowers you to let go of the outcome. So, the key to the third part of the strategy is to run hard after Plan A with great self-discipline—by design, not by default—all the while keeping your Plan C commitment in keen view.

Over the years, my family and friends have experienced several Plan C life events—from my sweet bride, Cindy, having difficult miscarriages early in our marriage to the hurricanes we Houstonians have endured that devastated so many Plan A pursuits. One year, my Plan A fitness vision to improve my tennis game was significantly disrupted when I stepped on a tennis ball, tearing ligaments in my ankle. In our financial firm, the loss of a key leader at a critical time had a significant effect on our best Plan A outcome.

Your answers in this three-part exercise, whatever they may be, will tell you what your optimal pursuits are. Once you've identified the summits that inspire you, determine what courageous contentment would look like for you. Together, we will then map out a course for getting to your summits, one step at a time.

OTHER WAYS TO THE END GOAL

Another way to get to your end goal and claim your summits is to detail side by side on a piece of paper: *How do I want to feel in the future?* And: *What do I absolutely not want to feel?* Don't type it on the computer; physically writing things out helps you reflect more deeply and think more productively.

If these two questions seem a little esoteric to you, then identifying what you do and don't like about your current life should help. Draw four columns on a sheet of paper. In the far-left column, list out your "likes." What elements of your job give you a sense of accomplishment? Whom do you enjoy seeing or talking to on a regular basis? Which activities on your calendar do you look forward to? Include your favorite hobbies and the things that relax you.

After you've made this list, read over it. Now, in the second column, beside each "like," write down why you like it. Avoid judging your answers; this isn't a right-or-wrong exercise. You have your reasons, and you can own them. In the third and fourth columns, do the same with your "don't likes." Itemize what is weighing you down and what you're not enjoying about your current life, and then write down why, one by one.

As the last step, grab another sheet of paper and do some brainstorming. The sky's the limit. Don't edit yourself or evaluate what's realistic in your situation. Just dream a little. Look one more time at your four lists and then, on this fresh sheet of paper—this clean slate—brainstorm ways to take the favorites from your "likes" list and turn them into something you love. What would enhance your life, making your "likes" even more appealing? What don't you like that you're ready to let go of?

For example, I know of a single mom in Minneapolis who identified what she really enjoyed about her job:

o   Working from home

o   Having freedom and flexibility in her schedule

o   Working closely with people in a meaningful way

o   Improving her home and seeing what others were doing with theirs

Dana (not her real name) *was* working from home with a small team of people in an entrepreneurial company that was providing an important service to its clients, yet she was miserable because she was doing two things she really didn't like: spending most of her time sitting at a desk, and focusing on numbers all day long. Because she hadn't been trained in accounting, not only was her creativity being squelched, but she felt the need to constantly quadruple-check her work so as not to make mistakes. This added a great deal of stress and meant longer hours on the job and less time with her two kids.

Once she figured out how to turn her "likes" into "loves," her dream job came into focus: pursuing a career as a real estate agent. And as soon as that destination was in view, she was able to work backward and plan out the individual steps to get there.

Here's another example: Very recently, Cindy and I had a wonderful brunch with close friends whose youngest daughter was graduating from college. We were celebrating their daughter's significant accomplishment alongside the happy reality that this couple was now free of college expenses. By having successfully seen their three children through college, they had essentially received a pay raise!

These circumstances had prompted a lot of thought for the

husband about how to maximize his future, and our brunch conversation soon turned to his work. He liked some aspects of his job, he told us, but there were three significant negatives:

1. A lack of flexibility in his vacation time
2. A boss who was less than ideal
3. A huge concern with the character and integrity of the company itself

He and his wife were able to arrive at an important decision that day: now that they would no longer be paying for college, the husband could resign from his position. Even if he didn't find a new job, they could live on the wife's income as long as they managed their expenses (by design, not by default). From there, the four of us discussed the things that the husband loves doing and the importance of the culture of any firm he might join, and we collectively landed on two or three great vocational possibilities for him in the future.

Life does give us opportunities to "trade up" in our pursuits. Having the vision to make that transition is an important element for both success and actually reaching our goals of significance.

EYES ON THE ROAD AHEAD

Besides envisioning worthy destinations, the other way we can keep living in the right direction is to keep our eyes on the road ahead.

Distracted driving is an epidemic in America. One extensive US

Department of Transportation study found that the person behind the wheel was responsible for an astounding 95 percent of motor vehicle accidents. And nearly three in four of those driver-caused accidents were due to distracted driving or decision errors such as misjudging what other drivers were doing.[3]

I think we could say much the same of our lives. Sometimes we crash because we are inexperienced and made a mistake. But more often, we end up in the ditch because we aren't focused on the road in front of us.

For almost everyone in the lead-yourself journey, the biggest distraction—by far—is what the people around us are doing. And just as surely as taking your eyes off the road can wreck your car, being overly focused on the world around you can wreck your dreams.

I'll say it straight: too many people are caught up in doing as others do. Some of them follow their friends' lead or comply with their parents' expectations. Other folks wander with the crowd or float along with the trends—and end up wherever the current takes them. Either way of life produces the same tragic result: settling for smaller goals than they should have had and a lesser life than they could have had.

We are not meant to meander! As Guy Finley has said, each of us has been "created with a possibility far greater than to merely appear and disappear as some form in the river of passing time."[4] I can't stress this enough. Again, it's absolutely no coincidence that we are born with two eyes and two feet facing in the same direction. Everything about our makeup reinforces the fact that we've been designed for...a life by design! We've been fashioned for forward movement and focused vision.

As I stated earlier in this chapter, where there is no vision, people perish. That statement comes from the Bible so I once again add, with a vision, often people thrive. Living without a vision—and especially a vision of your own that aligns with your distinct design—probably won't kill you, but it will almost certainly prove fatal to your dreams. With a vision, all kinds of things become possible. I learned this in a very surprising way.

College students are among my favorite people to spend time with. I've not only taught a long-standing leadership class at Baylor University, but for several years, I was invited to give a signature talk to each new crop of seniors at Texas A&M's school of business. My central message to college seniors is that you will encounter a lot of things to bet on in the future—things like the economy or a fad or a business start-up—but your best investment is to "bet on yourself." As a part of this talk, I ask the students to write down their future dreams for their marriage, their vocation, their health and fitness, their spiritual growth, and their community involvement. The exercise is usually met with such enthusiasm that I have to interrupt their feverish writing so we can move on to the next category.

This activity worked so well with the students that I thought I would try it with the older adults I also had the opportunity to speak to, who were typically in their forties and fifties. I didn't continue it for long, though, because each time, my older audiences quickly grew irritated; they huffed and crossed their arms, and cocked their heads sideways as if to say, "Doesn't this joker know that dreams don't come true?"

The exercise that had been so invigorating to twentysomethings was frustrating and futile to the seasoned "veterans of life." Why? What happens between the ages of twenty-two and forty-two? I didn't get to talk with each of the adults personally, but based on my innumerable conversations with company clients over the years, I'd speculate that for some in those audiences, the school of hard knocks has suppressed their dreams, or fear has consumed their hopes, convincing them that bold vision is the fairy dust of youth, not real life. For the majority of them, though, their choices to follow the crowd and fit in at all costs have caused them to gradually lose their way. And that lostness has produced a listlessness, an apathy, in adulthood that has made their dreams seem impossibly far away.

I was saddened by the cynicism of those adults. At the same time, their reactions put an even greater fire in me to write this book—because not even an eighty-two-year-old should be living in surrender, much less a forty-two-year-old. A life of significance always gives us something to strive for...at any age. And it is always, *always* attainable as long as we look and live in the right direction.

Once a person has realized the need to fix their eyes in the right direction, they look into their hearts, find their passions—and pursue them. Crafting a life based on the truth of who they are and all that they can do, a journey specific to their attributes and what they were created to accomplish, they suddenly find the gas pedal. As they identify their talents and callings, almost nothing can hold them back. And out of all that insight comes better foresight, a clearer view of where they're going.

With that foresight, that vision, determining an Immediate Action Plan to reach their destination comes rather naturally. This entails first taking small steps in the direction of the summit to form a routine or habit. This is Stage 2 of every traveler's Master Action Plan, and it will be our focus in the pages ahead.

WITH EYES WIDE OPEN

Before we exit this chapter, I want to share about a friend of mine who exemplifies everything we've been talking about here. If anyone was ever known for going after his goals with a singular focus, it would be NFL and Pro Football Hall of Fame linebacker Mike Singletary. Players and fans alike remember Mike not only for his intensity and his intelligence, but for his wide-open, glaring eyes on game day. Someone once asked him why he played with his eyes so wide. "Because I didn't want to miss anything," he said, "any clues indicating where the ball might be headed."

There was a time, though, when he wasn't so intent on knowing what was next. He was the youngest of ten kids, growing up poor in Houston, in a home rife with conflict between his parents. The marriage eventually ended, and Mike's dad remarried and had other kids. Before Mike was in his teens, two of his siblings died, including an older brother who was a father figure to him.

By the age of twelve, Mike Singletary had reached his limit, and he gave up. But his version of quitting was this: "I'm not going to be the worst; I'm not going to be the best. I'm just going to stay in the middle. Mediocre is great."

His mom, however, had a different vision for her son's future. "I need you to step up and be the man of the house," she told him. "I see something very special in you. There's a reason why you're here."

"And that was the day," Mike says, "that I walked in my room and got out a sheet of paper and wrote out my vision statement." Here's what Mike wrote:

Get a scholarship to college.

Get my degree.

Become an All-American.

Get drafted and go to the NFL.

Become an All-Pro.

Go to the Super Bowl.

Buy my mom a house.

Own my own business.

His youthful View of the Summit inspired a twelve-year NFL career. The child who nearly sentenced himself to the middle of the pack became a man determined to reach the pinnacle and be the best. And though the challenges kept coming, he kept his eyes on the prize.

Baylor was the only major college to offer him an athletic scholarship, and he paid them back in wins and All-American honors. Once his college football days were done, Mike's favorite team, the Cowboys, passed on him in the 1981 NFL draft, despite Mike's coach, Grant Teaff, telling legendary Dallas coach Tom Landry: "This guy will take you to the Super Bowl." Landry listened instead to his player guru, who deemed Mike—who was just under six feet tall—too short for NFL success.

Nevertheless, Mike devoted himself to his goals, and every element of Mike's vision for himself came true:

Get a scholarship to college (Baylor University). ✓

Get my degree (bachelor's and master's). ✓

Become an All-American (three times). ✓

Get drafted and go to the NFL (second round, 1981, thirty-
eighth player overall, chosen by the Chicago Bears). ✓
Become an All-Pro (ten times). ✓
Go to the Super Bowl (starting middle linebacker for the
Chicago Bears, Super Bowl XX champions). ✓
Buy my mom a house. ✓
Own my own business. ✓

As often happens when we dream big and hold to it, Mike went on to accomplish even more than he envisioned. Not only was he the league's Defensive Player of the Year twice during his career, but he was selected to the Pro Football Hall of Fame in his first year of eligibility.

Mike lived his vision of success in a way that few others ever have. But his family paid a price. Because his focus was football, he wasn't as present at home with his wife, Kim, and their kids. After his retirement following the 1992 season, Kim told him, "For years, you've had your helmet on and your vision was limited." Once he removed the helmet for good, that was "the first time that he could really see everything."

Realizing the shortsightedness of his vision, Mike turned his sights toward a significantly greater summit: that of being the best father and husband he could be. And at his induction into the Pro Football Hall of Fame five years later, Kim stood at the podium and said of the man she'd married, "Everyone knows he deserved to be in the Hall of Fame [as a player]. But he really is a Hall of Fame dad and Hall of Fame husband. He really, truly is." His approach to the game is how he has approached his life: with an intensity that has kept him on course to his dreams and a vision so clear that he saw every summit before he reached it.[5]

Mike Singletary has led himself well. As a result, he became a leader of leaders. His life demonstrates how forming a vision and then following it can catapult you from survival or success to the stratosphere of significance in multiple areas of your life. If he could develop a vision for himself at age twelve, and then refine that vision two decades later, absolutely nothing can stop you, either.

The questions we've explored in these two chapters are the ones you need to get your journey underway. They are the questions of not just a lead-yourself life but the beginnings of a legacy—the first moves toward what I hope will be several summits of significance in your lifetime. Cast your sights in that direction and keep your eyes on *your* road. The best is just ahead.

CHAPTER 7

STUCK

It's wise to make plans for our lives, but it's important to remember that life doesn't always turn out the way we've planned. Remember Plan A, Plan B, and Plan C? Sometimes, after climbing the heights of success or achieving a hallmark experience of significance, we find ourselves suddenly knocked off our feet, tumbling back to base camp, wondering what just happened.

An especially important time to keep leading ourselves is when we're face-to-face with more than a momentary challenge, because this is when a lot of people get stuck. Rather than fighting their way out or figuring their way out, they decide to just sit things out and wait in hopes that their circumstances will change. Yet this is the time we most need a plan, a strategy. Sometimes it will be an escape plan, and sometimes it will be an endurance plan until we can dig our way out—but we want an exit strategy nonetheless.

In this chapter, we will explore two "survival scenarios" that most commonly trip people up, stranding them and their dreams. After all, awareness is your first line of defense. Then, in the next chapter, we'll talk about how to get unstuck no matter how you got there.

HAWAII RESCUE

I only wish I'd had leading myself in mind when Cindy and I were on our honeymoon to Hawaii in 1987! I was so grateful to have married such a wonderful girl, but the truth is, I was really broke and couldn't afford the trip. Still, upon arriving at the airport in Maui, I decided to upgrade our rental car to a four-wheel-drive Jeep with a retractable roof. I so wanted our honeymoon to be a memorable start to our life adventure together, and it seemed to me that some fun wheels would be a great symbol of that hope.

For our week in Hawaii, we planned a coastal excursion: we would drive the road to Hana. Hana Highway's sixty-plus miles weave through hundreds of curves, across dozens of bridges, and past a veritable paradise of scenery—everything from high cliffs and verdant valleys to waterfalls, state parks, and beaches with white, black, or even red sand. Cindy and I packed food for a picnic, expecting to make it an all-day outing.

Somewhere along the way, I impetuously took an opportunity to go off-roading. Within about fifteen minutes, the rough dirt road that I chose led us out to a deserted beach along the ocean. Surrounded by water, volcanic rock faces, tropical vegetation, and sand as far as the eye could see, this seemed the perfect place to show my new bride what a fearless adventurer she'd married. Although Cindy was hesitant, I ignored her warnings that maybe this wasn't a good idea and announced, "Hold on tight, honey!" Then I hit the gas, cranked the wheel, and started doing doughnuts that would've made my sixteen-year-old self proud.

We spun and spun, kicking up sand and laughing and screaming like two kids on a roller coaster. In my bravado, I failed to notice that with each completed circle, we were inching closer to the water. Even though the sand was getting thicker and the Jeep less responsive, I kept pushing the limits, confident in our four-wheel drive and in my skills.

In retrospect, I was far too confident. In retrospect, I should've quit while I was ahead. But rather than being content that I'd had my fun and gotten to show off a little for my bride, you can guess what happened: it wasn't long before our tires got hung up in the damp sand along the water's edge. I didn't just hang us up a little. I got the vehicle stuck so badly that the wheels were buried to the axles!

After several attempts at pushing the Jeep out with Cindy at the wheel, it was apparent that we were not going anywhere. So, there we were—in those days before cell phones—helplessly stuck on a desolate beach, in the tropical heat with the sun beating down on us, with no help in sight. I was not only embarrassed, but I felt I had spoiled our honeymoon adventure day.

We did eventually receive rescue. After maybe an hour and a half, another couple in a Jeep (this one with a winch) noticed our plight from way up above on the road, and they eased their way down that treacherous dirt path and onto the beach to pull us out. Cindy and I made it to Hana and had our picnic, a little worse for the wear and much later than expected, but we were back on course, thanks to those gracious fellow travelers.

SURVIVAL SCENARIO #1:
THE CRISIS YOU CAUSE

There's more than one way to get stuck, but the most regretful is when we do it to ourselves—the self-made crisis. That's why, in the lead-yourself adventure, goal number one is: *do everything within your means to avoid getting stuck in the first place.*

I'll be the first to admit, Cindy's and my situation wasn't dire; we knew that someone would come along to help us eventually, and in the meantime, we had food, water, and the shelter of the Jeep. But there have been—and are even now—plenty of times when, if I don't lead myself to think ahead and choose wisely, I could put our marriage or even our lives in jeopardy—physically, financially, or emotionally. And though Cindy and I have laughed often about our little escapade in the years since, I haven't forgotten its sobering lesson: on that day, I put not just myself but the woman I love in a position where we were completely stuck and *needlessly* dependent on rescue from someone else.

Obviously, accidents and tragedies do occur, and then we are necessarily (and gratefully) reliant on others. But if I'm intent on leading myself, I need to eliminate any unnecessary risks. That means forgoing foolhardy, reckless decisions that wedge me, my loved ones, or my team at work into a helpless spot. I also must forgo the mental sinkholes and behavioral traps that can keep me spinning my wheels. This is the stuff that, if we're not careful, can hang us up before we know it.

Life gives us two options: either accept our circumstances or work to change them. There are certain things we cannot change, but our attitude and outlook are never on that list. Let's be agents for change by avoiding default mind-sets and behaviors.

Default Mind-Sets. There is a pair of default mind-sets—mental pitfalls—that can drag you down and keep you down. The first is a *victim mentality.* You never come out ahead as long as you're playing the blame or shame game. Blame says, "I'm the victim of someone or something else"; shame says, "I've victimized myself." Either way, such thinking won't help you up and out of tough circumstances. Because I am choosing to be the "victim," I do not take personal responsibility and own the future. In fact, it makes matters worse by inclining you to self-sabotage. You're much more likely to overlook opportunities, squander resources, or surrender to defeat. And when you do, where are you when tomorrow comes? Stuck where you started, hoping someone will come to your rescue. But there are no victims in the lead-yourself realm. No matter how you got stuck, there are things you can do to pull yourself out and make a success of your setbacks. The ideas in the next chapter will help.

The second default mentality is a *scarcity mentality.* There will inevitably be times when life drops you in unfamiliar territory with only limited supplies. In those survival scenarios, will you look around to see how you can make what you *do* have work even better? Or will you focus on what you're missing and who has it better than you?

You'll hear plenty of people claim they can't get unstuck because they are minus something: *I'm just not getting the breaks at work. My boss doesn't like me. We aren't making enough money for me to go back to school and get my master's degree. I never know how to approach girls; I'm too shy.* Others will tell you they got off course because life has been unkind: *If only my parents hadn't divorced…If only I hadn't been bullied…If only my ex hadn't drunk so much…*It's possible you've been sucked into such scarcity thinking yourself. Anyone who claims they can't lead themselves because they're minus *something*—that's fear talking, not the truth. Believing you lack what you need to succeed at anything—overcoming obstacles, building healthy relationships, achieving financial security, living out your dreams—is a sure route to self-sabotage and, consequently, to a defeated life.

Yet it's unnecessary because, I can promise you: *none of us come to our journey on this planet unequipped.* Whether you *live* by design or not, you have *been* designed with everything you need for the individual journey you're supposed to take. In fact, you're not missing anything that you need (except maybe the know-how that is in this book). You have a skill set and background custom-made for the varied and uncommon adventures that will be on your MAP.

In Lynne Twist's excellent book *The Soul of Money* is a chapter entitled "What You Appreciate Appreciates."[1] This is a lesson she learned from her travels around the world, visiting impoverished people in places where the most basic resources—food, money, and water—are truly scarce. Somehow, though, an abundance mentality exists in these environments that is rarely seen in our modern culture. These people who have nothing by worldly standards are eager to open their homes, their lives, and their hearts, and share whatever they do have with strangers and loved ones alike. They are not consumed with "What's in it for me?" thinking as so many of us are.

How can this be? How can people with scarce resources be virtually unconcerned with questions of "Will there be enough?," while those of us who live in relative luxury lie awake at night worrying that we're falling behind our competition or losing status within our social network? Because the opposite is also true: what you don't appreciate depreciates. As Twist explains, "When your attention is on what's lacking and scarce—in your life, in your work, in your family, in your town—then that becomes what you're about. That's the song you sing, the vision you generate. You engage in lack and longing and what's missing, and you call others to that same experience." And if you live in that mind-set long enough, Twist says, no matter what you do have, it will never be enough, even though you undoubtedly have *more* than enough to escape any difficulty you're in.[2]

The problem with such default thinking or behavior is that it limits your sights. You get tunnel vision the longer you live there, seeing only the immediate trouble around you, not the sky above you or the vistas beyond you. Rather than the inspiration of the long view (and the sustained significance it represents), the desperation of the short view takes over. *Me* and *now* become the focus. And as long as you're bound up in these, you won't ever achieve your peak existence.

Significance is neither shortsighted nor selfish. It's not just "all about me" or "all about now." The journey to significance requires diligently keeping an eye toward avoiding getting stuck, in order to go the distance and benefit others.

Default Behaviors. Having spent my career conducting personal inventories to help people define their goals so that I and my company can best serve their objectives, I've gained some insight into the kinds of things that can stop an adventure in its tracks. What is it that keeps people stuck in default, spinning their wheels, sinking ever deeper into the quicksand of lost opportunity? First and foremost, we see these ditches in default behaviors, such as the following:

- *Vices.* Whereas virtues are life-giving habits, vices are life-draining habits. Do you have any vices that are hindering your forward progress? Don't only consider the obvious ones such as excessive drinking or gambling. We also may "stick" ourselves by living beyond our financial means.

By laziness. By not listening to people who know better than we do. Or by eating too much or otherwise not taking care of our health.

- *Dark secrets.* Because every aspect of our lives is interconnected, what remains hidden, what we're afraid to tell, what we do when we think no one will find out, is especially dangerous. The burden of carrying a secret or living a double life—whether it's an affair, internet pornography, or dishonest business practices—not only weighs you down, but it may well lead to a very public downfall that could hinder your journey to success and prevent you from ever reaching significance. Darkness is dark.

- *Toxic relationships or settings.* Ever meet someone who was in a really difficult, debilitating situation that they simply would not leave? They continued to swim laps in toxic waters, simply because it was familiar, and they were scared of change. Relationships exist out there that are deeply damaging. We must courageously choose to look truth in the eye and make radical change when it's necessary.

Your struggles may be different from the ones I've mentioned here. Still, with any default behavior that is keeping you down, my appeal to you is the same: please give yourself the gift of help. If you can't help yourself out of your current hole—can't discern the way out or are lacking the skills or self-discipline to get yourself out—then seek help from others who know the way. (This is still leading yourself, because you're taking action on your own behalf to move forward.) Admit what you're dealing with—starting with yourself—and then tell someone else.

Denial or excuses won't set you free. They are nothing more than lies in disguise. Likewise, avoiding the pain of reality isn't really avoiding it; you're simply burying it for a time where it is sure to resurface later. Admit it so you can quit it, and then seek accountability in the way that works for you: enlist the support of your spouse or best friend, hire a coach, or get therapy or group support, either online or in person. Go to whatever lengths you must to shine healing light on the dark places in your life. As soon as you do, you'll again see forward movement.

CHECK THE DOWNSIDE

In the previous chapter, we discussed the need for capturing the View of the Summit for any goal on your journey. This helps you as you seek to ascend from survival to success to significance. The "downside" of the journey is important to forecast as well. I refer to it as the *View of Disaster*. Evaluate:

o   What path are you currently on that could derail your dreams?
o   What choices are compromising your traction?
o   Are you tiptoeing along the edge of a precipice?
o   Do you know where the quicksand is?

We tend to rationalize or diminish these hazards, telling ourselves, "This shouldn't even be a concern," or, "That won't affect me." Often, we deny that we're on a destructive path at all. Yet we can predict with certainty that particular paths will lead to difficulty, hard times, possibly even heartache or ruin. It's pure physics—*life* physics:

o The deeper you sink, the harder it is to get out.

o If you do nothing to prevent a fall, you can expect to follow a downward trajectory from bad to worse...to worst.

o Once you're falling, there's no stopping your momentum without herculean effort. In no time flat, a descent can become a rockslide. And rockslides don't stop until they've hit bottom.

So, as a general rule, be on the lookout for where the footing is treacherous or the path unsafe—and don't go there! Not to be Captain Obvious here, but your best safeguard is to distance yourself from the sinkholes and the sheer drops that you know are there. Then, build steps into your Master Action Plan (see part 3 of this book) that will keep you away from those trouble spots, as well as the ones you aren't aware of.

SURVIVAL SCENARIO #2:
THE CRISIS YOU CAN'T SEE COMING

Sometimes you get stuck because you've been careless. You've either set off into a venture (marriage, education, job, parenting) without a plan at all, or you've departed from the plan, as I did so impulsively on Cindy's and my honeymoon. But there's another type of stuck that produces a lot of fear, and the opening scene of the hit movie *The Blind Side* illustrates it well.

If you're one of the millions of people who have watched the Oscar-nominated film, you probably still remember that poignant moment. It replays actual NFL game footage of New York Giants linebacker Lawrence Taylor's career-ending hit on Washington Redskins quarterback Joe Theismann. Taylor's blind-side tackle of Theismann, which ranks among the most devastating collisions in National Football League history, bore so much force—literally and figuratively—that it changed the way football teams operate on and off the field to this day.

Though I never played quarterback during my football-playing days in high school and college, I was on the painful end of more than a few never-saw-them-coming hits as a wide receiver. I won't ever forget one particular hit during practice, from my own teammate at Baylor, Mike Singletary. (Yes, *that* Mike Singletary from chapter 5.) It was my freshman year of college. I was on the scout team, and Mike was already a two-time college All-American linebacker. The scout team would run the upcoming opponent's plays to give the defense a look at what to expect. This particular play had the wide receiver (me) going across the middle on a shallow slant route. A wobbly pass came my way, and I jumped to catch it. As I was coming down, Mike was coming up, and I took the brunt of the hit. Honestly, he wasn't even going full speed, yet that tackle left me gasping for air and out of commission!

In one sense, life isn't much different from football: everyone who ever steps on the field *will* get blindsided eventually, only minus the helmet and pads. Hits happen to the All-Americans and the members of the scout team, the cameramen and the coaches, even the water boys and the players in the marching band. These hits set us back. Knock the breath out of our bodies. And force us to the ground.

One of the most significant blindsides in my own life came during a corporate meeting that I was chairing in 2006. The boardroom in Milwaukee was packed, and we'd had some intense conversation regarding our firm's national expansion. Partway through the meeting, a woman rushed into the back of the room and said, "Mr. Reeter, please gather your belongings and come with me. There's been an emergency." With my mind reeling, I followed her into the hallway, where she explained, "Your father has had a stroke. We've made arrangements for you to fly to Missouri to be with him. Your flight leaves in an hour." Shortly after, I was sitting at my father's bedside in intensive care as he took his last breaths.

More blindsides packed a one-two punch several years later. In the span of ten days, my precious mother-in-law, Mimi, and my older brother, Joel, were each diagnosed with cancer; Mimi's cancer was terminal within six months. Joel's ordeal has been going on ever since. With just a few words, their doctors sent each of them and our entire family into survival mode. Instantly.

I know plenty of others who have been left dazed by astonishing hits. A young financial adviser in our firm comes to mind—a solid husband and amazing daddy whose wife abruptly declared, "I don't love you anymore. I want a divorce." My pastor, H. Edwin Young, has gone through it, too. One day he was thriving with significant worldwide impact as the leader of a Houston megachurch with eighty thousand–plus members, and then, suddenly, he was in crisis mode with his wonderful wife, Jo Beth, fighting for her life.

I'm sure you could add some blindsides of your own to this list. Coronavirus, economic decline, and social distancing. Maybe your best friend betrayed you. Or you've been laid off from your job with no warning. Or you have a prodigal child who took to the streets without a word of good-bye.

The ones that can stop you cold are the ones you don't see coming. No one is immune to these crises, no area of our lives is off-limits. Our vocation, finances, faith, family, friendships, even our mental toughness, will all likely be challenged at different times in our lives. And while you can't thoroughly prepare for these, at least be aware that the blindsides *will* come. It may seem counterintuitive, but it does help to acknowledge and expect that there will be life-altering shifts and downturns. To not be surprised by suffering is one secret to enduring it and to ultimately leading yourself out of it.

Another secret is to prepare *yourself.* With life's blindsides, there's no telling what you might one day be up against, so preparing for a particular scenario is tough. My own experience has shown that, even if you know a hit is coming—that you're going to lose a loved one to a terminal illness, for example—it's still impossible to anticipate all the ways that situation will affect you. Nothing can completely prepare you for losing someone you love. Still, there are internal resources you can develop and practice right now that can produce a positive outcome and see you through those trials.

The real tragedy is not to be faced with tragedy, but to miss the opportunity to overcome it—to miss your greatest adventure—because you weren't ready to rise to the occasion. You can't plan for each and every possible scenario, but you can work to be your best self for when your best self is needed. The stronger your internal resources, the better equipped you'll be to come up with a winning exit strategy in the worst of times.

Need a few ideas for preparing yourself? Read insightful books.

Journal. Practice the art of thankfulness. Find a life coach, mentor, therapist, or pastor. Pray. Exercise. Eat right. Speak truth and life to yourself. Let your mind dwell on things that are true, honorable, right, pure, lovely, admirable, praiseworthy, and/or of good report. Surround yourself with encouraging people. Strengthen your mind and heart, not just your body, with daily disciplines. And always, always keep feeding the fires of hope and faith. We will talk about some of these things in more detail in the chapters ahead.

SURVIVING THE SHIFTS

Even if we're leading ourselves, life will occasionally propel us from success or significance back to survival. There will be seasons in which we are thriving in certain areas and then, in an instant, our "thrive" will be disrupted. We saw this on a national level early in the new millennium. Americans felt relatively safe and secure on September 10, 2001, but by 11 a.m. on 9/11, everything had changed. A few weeks after that fateful day, I received a call from Coach Teaff. He challenged me to step up and told me that my country needed me to be a leader. That call from my mentor and friend was not only timely but highly impactful for me.

Sometimes the downturns are beyond our control, as on that fateful day for our country. Other times, they are absolutely within our control. My point here is: don't put yourself in the ditch if you can help it. We're going to experience crises no matter what—it's the nature of life on this earth—but if we're not leading ourselves, we will undoubtedly experience them a lot more often. Let's eliminate the "stuck" we can control, so that our energies can be focused on dealing effectively with the kind that can't be avoided.

ARE YOU STUCK?

Survival scenarios are known for making us feel down and out, but as long as you're leading yourself, you're never down for the count. A sure way to pave the way to significance is by pinpointing the places where you might be stuck. This knowledge will help you construct appropriate exit strategies and come out ready to blaze new trails. Just take a few moments to examine your everyday thoughts. Mark which, if any, of the following statements you say, feel, or think on a regular basis.

- o "I'm not really happy."
- o "I'm bored."
- o "I'm numb."
- o "I'm always tired."
- o "I hate my job."
- o "I'm pessimistic about..."
- o "I'm not big on change, even positive change."
- o "I can't leave because..."
- o "I don't really have any goals."
- o "Dreams are for suckers/the naive/the young."
- o "I could never succeed at that."
- o "What's everybody else doing?"
- o "I don't feel like it."
- o "There's no point."
- o "I have nothing to offer."
- o "I don't have what it takes."
- o "I can't do that because..."

- o "If only..."
- o "I'll just wait until..."
- o "It is what it is."

Now, go back through the list and write down three to five of the statements that you use most frequently. In the right margin after each of those, write down which area of your life comes first to mind. It could be a relationship, your job, your finances, your health and fitness, even matters of faith. Your answers here will help you identify not only where you're stuck but where to focus your efforts to get moving again. And if, after all of this, you're still not sure if you're spinning your wheels, ask somebody who's close to you: "Where do you think I'm stuck?"

CHAPTER 8

═══════════════

GETTING UNSTUCK

There's no question that life is fraught with hazards and obstacles that leave us vulnerable. Nevertheless, living by design means not only avoiding getting stuck but coming out of our challenges stronger than before. The secret is found in what one former NFL head coach used to say to his players: "Don't tell me what you can't do. Just tell me what you won't do."[1]

A reluctance to exercise all reasonable possibilities in a survival scenario is what often keeps people stuck. Are you willing to do the work to get unstuck?

DO SOMETHING!

It's possible you've been stuck in survival mode without realizing it: existing but not experiencing what your life has to offer, or tackled by hardship, face still planted in the turf. Whether you're in physical survival mode due to an illness, emotional survival mode due to a divorce, or financial survival mode due to a job loss, don't just sit there. Strategize! Fight! Put yourself to work! There is always something you can do to get back up and keep moving forward.

Robert Lewis, the founder of Men's Fraternity, says that we must reject the passivity that seems to creep into our lives as we get older. To reject passivity means to choose, or accept, activity and a can-do spirit. You'll find that all kinds of extraordinary things happen—all kinds of obstacles can be overcome—simply because you're willing to do whatever it takes to once again pursue your vision.

How does that work? The principle is straightforward: doing something does something! To get off the couch and start working toward a worthwhile goal produces change within us as well as alters our environment. Doing something positive—anything positive—will help; but put together a string of productive and meaningful actions in your circumstance, and you'll soon find yourself back on level footing, ready to keep trekking toward higher ground. That's the nature of leading yourself. Keeping your "won't do" list short means your "can't do" list will practically disappear altogether.

PUSH FOR SIGNIFICANCE

I'm very aware of how hard this can be. I have dear friends who were born "in the woods," so to speak—subject to someone else's careless choices or to adverse circumstances that were not of their own making. I know of others who have been leveled by a massive, unexpected challenge that they're desperately trying to dig out from under; and others yet who are in way over their heads because they made choices that have put themselves in harm's way. One thing is true for all of them: a moment comes when they must decide to either try to fight their way free or to stay where they are and forfeit their most amazing future.

When you find yourself buried by an avalanche, you need to get up and do *something*, as we've said—start digging out with your bare hands if necessary! It not only keeps you from the defeat of staying stuck in survival mode, but it virtually guarantees that you're going to see daylight again.

I urge you, though, to do more than strive for daylight. *Once you've dug out, head for higher ground and rebuild.* This is goal number two for the hard times in your lead-yourself journey. Rebuilding on higher ground will look different for each of us, but it's all about redeeming those difficult life experiences. Arriving at a better place because of what we've been through. Creating a greater outcome than we would have otherwise. Rising above "I'm glad to be alive" and pressing on to significance.

Remember the early days of the coronavirus seclusion. In many ways that felt like an avalanche. Over weeks and months, though, we saw different people dealing with it in different ways. For sure there will be lasting effects from that difficulty, but those who chose proactively to dig out and move forward got unstuck.

Bob Smith is a financial adviser at our firm. He, his wife, Jeannie, and their daughter, Jessica, lost their home in Hurricane Harvey. For a brief time afterward, they lived with Cindy and me, and we were both struck by their positive energy and optimism as a family. It was truly inspirational. Months later, they rebuilt their home on the same spot, but with an elevated foundation. The Smiths literally built on higher ground.

Another story from significance to survival and back is that of

Chuck Schoolcraft—my father-in-law, Cindy's dad. Chuck and Edna were married for fifty-six years. It was one of the most blissful, remarkable marriages I've ever witnessed. Edna, or as we called her, Mimi, completely spoiled Chuck! As I mentioned previously, she was diagnosed with stage four pancreatic cancer. Within months, on Thanksgiving 2015, she had passed. Everyone in our family had instant anxiety for Chuck's well-being, given the closeness of their relationship and how attentive to him Mimi had been. Chuck spent time in survival mode for sure. Then, gradually, he climbed out of the depths of despair and chose to move forward. Recently (a little over four years later), we spent Christmas in Beaver Creek, Colorado, with Chuck, whom we call Geedad, and our family. He shared that at age eighty-one, he has found meaning in being here for the growth and development of his grandchildren. He is such a special and vital part of our sons' lives; it is astonishing. He is a key part of their development into outstanding young men. Cindy and I are so grateful for his courageous, significant choice of pouring himself into the future of our children, his grandchildren.

If the person in crisis is concerned with any question, it is usually, *How do I get out of this?* Unfortunately, "getting out" can mean any number of things, including shutting down, giving up, or going backward, none of which will lead to a better place. The person who is striving for significance asks, *How do I redeem this?* That's the right question, even if you're in a situation you can't escape. Your circumstances may have you pinned to the mat, but your mind and heart don't need to lie there.

I often speak of my goals for the year, and how I intend for this year to be better than last year. One time, after giving a motivational speech on making it the best year of your life, a guy confronted me:

"You can't choose for one year to be better than any other year. Let's say I get cancer. What then?"

"If it was the last year of your life, how would you live it?" I cautiously responded. That's how you get unstuck. That's how you rise above what tries to bury you. I've learned so much from my brother who *does* have cancer. It's terminal. Yet each day, he assesses how he can rise above his circumstances and respond in ways that will outlive him. On one particularly difficult day, he remarked, "I had several really good minutes today."

I can say the same of Joe White. He is the president and owner of Kanakuk Kamps. He and his wife, Debbie Jo, are two of Cindy's and my closest friends, and their hearts are gold. Joe has invested himself in several national programs that make a positive difference in the lives of others. He was a keynote speaker at Promise Keepers, has spoken on college campuses across America through a program called AfterDark, and has challenged men to mentor and disciple one another through a ministry called Men at the Cross. Joe and Debbie Jo also founded a camp, Kids Across America, which brings thousands of inner-city kids to the Ozark Mountains to discover a different vision for life beyond gangs and violence. Joe does all of this while living with leukemia. In the past few years, he has also endured prostate cancer, open-heart surgery, and neuropathy in his lower extremities, which recently forced the amputation of his lower leg. Yet the guy has zero complaints. He truly lives each day of life as if it were his last. However, if you know Joe at all, you know he was doing that long before being diagnosed with leukemia.

We can and should be doing the same, because we all are "terminal"—we all have an expiration date ahead. Some of us will reach the deadline sooner than others; nevertheless, the push for significance can continue until our last breath.

DIG OUT

Of course, before you can seek significance, you must dig out from the sinkhole of survival mode. Here are some ways to do that.

Engage your mind, not your fears. When wilderness experts get lost or stuck, rather than wasting energy in a mindless frenzy (doing for doing's sake), they pause to get their bearings so they can conserve their energy for efforts that will matter.

As soon as you realize you're in trouble, instructs Charley Shimanski of the Mountain Rescue Association, "the most important thing you can do is S.T.O.P. (Sit, Think, Observe and Plan). Do not run off frantically looking for a way out…stop and assess your situation! Use your head, not your feet. At this point your brain is your most important piece of survival gear." Most wilderness fatalities occur, he says, because of the decisions that people make in the first ten minutes of a desperate situation.[2] In other words, reacting in fear isn't the answer. It digs your rut deeper. Those who panic are the least likely to make it out.

As you read in chapter 1, when I got lost in the Uncompahgre National Forest, I panicked and sped up. Bad idea! Thankfully, I paused to collect myself and mentally run through my options, and then I strategically started working to get myself out. My brother, Joel, and Joe White have done that, too. Both men devised a plan to avoid getting stuck in default thinking or behavior. They strategized how to move forward with hope and purpose in the reality of their diagnoses and maximize whatever time they had left. Their plans not only included great medical providers (such as MD Anderson and the Mayo Clinic), but also a mental attitude toward maximizing life during difficulty.

People who live by design do this. They might temporarily lose their way; they might get stuck for a while. Nevertheless, they will apply their minds to methodically and safely devise an escape plan. They may not be able to escape their circumstances, but escaping being stuck? That is always possible.

I understand that among the hardest parts of being in a period of survival is battling the range of volatile emotions that come with crisis territory. Those battles compound the difficulty of the experience. But if you can win the battles with yourself—especially the battle over fear—almost nothing can defeat you.

There's a reward for conquering this particular foe: overcoming what you are afraid of often proves to be the bridge to your success. The life-giving dreams and completed goals you're striving for lie just beyond your fears. But you have to be willing to stand up and push past what scares you.

Let nothing go to waste. Wilderness experts are also quick to take stock of their supplies and figure out what they can put to use. In those survival moments, their question is not one of scarcity or victimization ("What do I wish I had?" or "Why don't I have better supplies?") but, "What do I have to work with?" Take the same approach yourself. Identify what resources you do have—not just material items but your courage, your faith, your family and friends, your determination—and figure out ways to put them to use to create positive change that can get you moving again. (I'm not talking about using people, but rather about asking them to come alongside you and help you during these times.)

Those who lead themselves understand that reaching significance does not depend on how much you have, or how good you have it, but on how well you use what's available to you. Again, wilderness experts figure out a plan with the strategic use of every resource in mind. Often, they're forced to make something out of almost nothing, and something more out of something small, until what was small becomes consequential. By using this strategy, they find a way to forge ahead.

What Lynne Twist says in *The Soul of Money* really captures the essence of maximizing your resources: "If your attention is on the capacity you have to sustain yourself and your family, and contribute in a meaningful way to the well-being of others, then your experience of what you have is nourished and it grows. Even in adversity, if you can appreciate your capacity to meet it, learn, and grow from it, then you create value where no one would have imagined it possible."[3]

That's a pretty good game plan for survival of any kind—to look to create value out of what most people see as rubbish. What you have on hand may seem so little as to be meaningless, so ordinary as to be useless. And yet, even the lint from your pockets, when held under a shard of glass directed at the sun, is enough to start a fire in a survival situation. And from that tiny flame you can create a torch in order to carry the fire with you.

In other words, it doesn't take much. But you do have to take what you have and put it to use. Any blessing you have, any advantage—even a small one—can be used to help yourself out of a survival scenario. And in the long run, those things will probably become some of the very tools or skills you will use to someday help others out of their crises.

Focus on what you can control; forget about what you can't. In times when you find yourself stuck, it would be easy either to criticize yourself for ending up in that position, or to be overly cautious in trying to get out. Survival scenarios can sometimes leave you questioning whether you have what it takes to do what's best for yourself. But what's past is past, and a new day is underway right now. Instead of being bound by regrets over what has been, or worrying over what is beyond your control in this current scenario, refocus yourself on the truth that *you* get to decide how you will handle this situation. Your thoughts and emotions are up to you; you don't have to mindlessly react or be held hostage by your fears and regrets. You can "take them prisoner," so to speak, and choose how to respond—thoughtfully, with purpose, not haphazardly, and not in a panic. When you choose to focus on what you can control, a beautiful thing happens: you will begin to see the opportunity in every setback. Are you seeing it in yours?

CONTROL ISSUES

Thoughtfully consider what your response will be in your current survival situation by answering these questions:

- o   What am I focusing on that is outside of my control?
- o   What is within my control right now?
- o   What resources do I have within reach?
- o   What can I do with what I have?
- o   What more can I do with my resources?

Exercise gratitude. Marcus Warner and Jim Wilder's book, *Rare Leadership*, speaks of the profound connection between gratitude and joy. Anytime we lose our spirit of thankfulness, we lose our joy.

We recently had Wilder speak at our firm. It was fascinating to hear the brain science around his concept of "returning to joy" quickly. With joy, our productivity skyrockets. And almost nothing challenges our gratitude more than getting stuck. So, while it's great to practice gratitude every day, it's particularly essential when we're in survival.

I'm not suggesting being thankful for the suffering itself. But do go on a treasure hunt of sorts. Count your blessings, being careful not to overlook the littlest ones. I start a new Life Book each year, where I love to journal big and small things I am grateful for. It probably seems nuts, but I often even write about difficult things.

Search out the character traits that are being strengthened in you as a result of this difficulty. Name the good things and good people that *are* in your life. Thankfulness is a tremendous antidote to tragedy or adversity.

Engage your faith. Landing in crisis does not mean living helplessly or hopelessly. In fact, it's an opportune time to put hope to work so that your faith finds its wings. You may know someone whose psychology was more debilitating than their tragedy: a neighbor who was so defeated by a divorce, for example, that their spirit has never recovered even though they are happily remarried. There is certainly a time for grieving and for sorrow, but faith actively remembers that good is coming. Faith also reminds us that we can make something good out of something awful.

Each day that you live, you have the opportunity to make the world a better place for yourself and for the people around you. It doesn't matter whether you're in rehab or in debt, sitting in a wheelchair or on a witness stand. You may be confined to a hospital bed, but that doesn't have to stop you from sending up prayers for people or offering others a word of encouragement. Greg Abbott is the epitome of this notion, saying, "You can't keep a good man down." As a young man, fresh out of law school, Greg was running through Memorial Park in Houston. During his run for fitness and pleasure, a tree fell on him, restricting him to a wheelchair for the rest of his life. Greg was instantly relegated to survival mode, laid up in the hospital. Remarkably, though, with a spirit of courage and a vision for what is possible (not what isn't possible), Greg began to rise. That wheelchair did not detain him. Greg rose to the place of governor of Texas, and he is literally one of the best governors in the history of the state.

One of the distinct advantages of leading yourself is that even in a metaphorical coal mine, your faith can still shine like a diamond. And faith is made manifest by getting up every morning and doing good, rather than perpetuating the darkness. Joe White gets this. My brother gets this. As a result, they each have the faith and the fight of a warrior.

From the early days of their diagnoses, these men declared, "I'm going to fight this as hard as I can for as long as I can!" And they're still alive, inspiring and challenging all of us who know them to fight the good fight in our own lives, whatever it might be. I have been dramatically inspired by the way Joe White has handled his recent amputation. His response? "It's God's leg. It's all good."

Let the truth set you free. In the days following his leukemia diagnosis, I distinctly remember Joe White increasing his speaking schedule in order to maximize his impact in our world with the time he had left. Your faith can likewise keep you moving toward significance, as long as that faith is based in truth. Hope minus truth is blind optimism, and blind optimists have hope only so long as they see a chance of rescue. But if rescue doesn't come—if that surgery isn't successful, or their "big break" audition doesn't pan out, or they don't find their soul mate on that dating app—then shallow hope easily gives way, like a sinkhole, to the hopelessness of despair.

With our team at the office as well as people that I life-coach, I share about the three "isms": pessimism, optimism, and realism. Here's what I believe: Pessimism never helps. It has no place in our life. Optimism, on the other hand, is a critical element of every successful (and certainly every extraordinary) life pursuit. Still, optimism without realism is never complete. Optimism must be coupled with a healthy dose of reality, for it is the truth that will set you free. It has been said, "A pessimist sees the difficulty in every opportunity, and an optimist sees the opportunity in every difficulty." In order to get unstuck, you have to see the opportunity correctly. You must accept what you can't change, acknowledging reality for what it is, and then let faith have the last word.

During the coronavirus pandemic, pessimism, uncertainty, sensationalism, and fear were pervasive. At our financial-services firm, our theme was Realistic Optimism. In that theme we sought to be aware of reality and truth, yet optimistic in the ultimate outcome as it related to our clients and ourselves.

I found a great example of this in best-selling author Jim Collins's epic book *Good to Great*. The principle he speaks of—which I summarize as *Confront the brutal facts yet never lose faith*[4]—is one we can apply to any time of crisis. Collins illustrates this using the experiences of Vietnam War veteran Vice Admiral Jim Stockdale. Stockdale was the highest-ranking US Naval officer held in Hỏa Lò Prison, which its residents derisively referred to as the Hanoi Hilton. He and his fellow captives were beaten, tortured, and kept isolated for weeks on end from 1965 until their release in 1973. Yet Stockdale never gave up hope; he even devised a tap code for communication among the prisoners, which became an invaluable means of quiet resistance and camaraderie in that horrific place.

Among the more powerful takeaways of Stockdale's story is that in times of adversity, "you must maintain unwavering faith that you can and will prevail in the end, regardless of the difficulties, *and at the same time* have the discipline to confront the most brutal facts of your current reality."[5] So what did this prisoner of war do? In his own words, he "never lost faith in the end of the story."[6] He didn't expect to be out of captivity by that first Christmas, for example, but he ultimately clung to the belief that he and his fellow captives would find a way out—or nobly die trying. And of the eleven POWs who went through this journey together, only one did not make it out alive.[7]

You may not prevail over cancer or whatever difficulty you're in. But you can prevail in your journey toward significance. Death never has to have the last word. And in the passionate pursuit of significance, it doesn't.

REDEMPTION

The people you've read about here are living proof that your ability to lead yourself isn't dictated by where you've landed or by how hard you've been hit. Life may take you somewhere different from where you expected, or the ground beneath you might temporarily shift. Nevertheless, you can determine to get unstuck and dig your way out.

Sadly, not everybody finds their way out. But the people who do aren't those who shrug, sigh, and say, "What will be, will be." They admit that they are struggling, but then they press in to the work at hand, get unstuck, and get going—aiming higher and higher after they've regained their footing.

Adversity may come at you like an avalanche at times, but it must not keep you down. At the point where you've hit bottom, you have to take measured action. In the midst of the storm, in the depths of the wilderness, at the base of the mountain where victory seems the most distant, you have to fight to get unstuck and then seek to redeem the difficulty.

The power of this truth had great clarity in 2017. Our corporate team has survived multiple hurricanes during my tenure in Houston. Hurricane Ike was bad, but Harvey was absolutely devastating. When Harvey flooded Houston, our team of over two hundred people was deeply affected. Although, thankfully, we suffered no fatalities in our immediate group, nearly everyone was impacted in one way or another through the trauma, the total disruption of everyday life, the property damage—and thirteen of our families suffered significant personal losses, some losing everything.

In the aftermath of the storm, while we were displacing water and removing drywall and debris from one another's homes and yards, I made a lot of mistakes as a leader. I told them that we were moving forward; I sought to remind them that we would ultimately prevail, that this would not defeat us. I repetitiously used the General Patton quote: "A good plan, violently executed now, is better than a perfect plan next week." What we were doing and saying was not perfect, but we were certainly moving forward.

But you know what? It wasn't my words that convinced them. Day by day, as they cleared the trees and trash in the mud and muck that this horrendous storm had hurled into people's lives, as they put their hands to the work and did what they could do, they saw that they didn't have to settle for survival. They could do something—make something—of even this mess.

What I'm most proud of is that when these courageous people seemed to be submerged by catastrophe—with lengthy power outages, a lack of food and clean water, highways shut down, emergency services unable to get through—they didn't stay down. They fought their way out of the floodwaters, and then, you know what they did? They untied their boats; lit flashlights; got hip waders, gas lamps, and candles; bought bottled water; and went looking for others to see where they could lend a hand. Disaster deluged them but it didn't defeat them. They took their sights off themselves, reached out to help others in need with pure water and the hand of hope, and thereby ignited a different outcome—a redemptive outcome.

Another remarkable thing happened through the difficulty of Harvey. Seeing so many people devastated—some of them without a financial strategy—our team further honed its values. In the months and years since the hurricane, our organization has doubled down and given away hundreds of financial plans, so that others can be ready for an uncertain future.

This is perhaps the most important move we can make after we've dug ourselves out, and frankly, even *as* we're digging ourselves out. *Reaching out* is how we begin to resurface. It's how we unbury ourselves from the rubble. It's the purest way to rise from the dust and start to rebuild on higher ground.

What about you? Are you neck-deep in something that wants to bury you alive? Has life sucked you into a sinkhole, drowned you in despair? Have your choices landed you in the ditch? Don't sit there shivering in hopes of a rescue. Don't stay stuck. Strategize, fight, and find your way out. Then reach out to give someone else a hand. That's when redemption can begin and significance becomes inevitable.

MIND OVER MATTER

It's not enough to avoid the survival mind-sets we looked at in the previous chapter; you want to actually cultivate a mind-set that puts you on track toward your goals. Whether you're in a self-made crisis or you've been blindsided, here's the by-design thinking that separates those who get back up from those who get stuck. Remind yourself of these things as often as you need to:

- o   *I am not a victim. Adversity takes aim at everyone.*
- o   *I have a future worth fighting for.*
- o   *I need to focus on what I can control, what I can do, and what I have at my disposal.*
- o   *I have everything I need to lead myself out of this mess.*
- o   *I can and will come out of this stronger than ever, and as I do, I'll help someone else out, too.*

PART THREE

PLAN THE COURSE, LIVE THE DREAM

CHAPTER 9

THE PASSIONATE PURSUIT

Now that you've thoughtfully eyed the summit and determined where you're headed, you'll want to put the additional elements of your Master Action Plan into…action, setting goals that are purpose driven, realistic, measurable, and impactful.

Your MAP involves three stages: (1) envision the summit, which you've already done; (2) create an Immediate Action Plan; and (3) draft a Daily Action Plan for each life category you care about, cataloging daily entries in your Life Book. Using this system that we have developed and taken thousands of people through, you can work backward to move toward the five-year summit vision you're striving for.

I perceive this entire adventure as a passionate pursuit to which we're giving every part of ourselves—heart, mind, and soul—daily over a lifetime. Such a monumental endeavor needs long-term strategies and disciplines combined with an Immediate Action Plan. So, throughout this final section of the book, I will present numerous ways for you to integrate your goals, values, beliefs, and habits in order to both plan your course and live your dreams.

I define this most passionate of pursuits as a *lifestyle of integrity combined with a daily routine.* My understanding of *integrity* doesn't only refer to moral fiber and honesty. Of course, you need character and good values, but you also need a comprehensive process that engages every part of yourself without throwing you off-balance. The origin of the word itself highlights this. In Latin, the base word of *integrity* is *integer*, which means being whole, not fractionated. We're seeking to build an integrated, whole life that is purposefully driven in our various worlds and relationships.

Choosing an annual theme helps me so much, and I recommend it for everybody. Once I have a theme in mind, such as the 2020 Vision I mentioned in chapter 4, I spend a lot of time strategically planning how to walk it out in each aspect of my life in the coming year. This is one of several methods I use to enjoy a life of uncommon adventures.

THEMES

- o   Beyond
- o   Push Up for Success
- o   B.O.L.D. Infinite Adventure
- o   50

- o   Warrior
- o   Arise Shine
- o   Life Adventure with God as My Guide
- o   LifeLightLove
- o   Ride Forth Victoriously

This whole-life mission is so essential that, in the horse barn at our family ranch, we've displayed the words to our family's favorite song, Steven Curtis Chapman's "The Great Adventure." When our boys were young and that song would come on the radio, Chad, Ryan, and Cody would energetically shout its opening line, "Saddle up your horses!" as they envisioned the ride of a lifetime. At the ranch, we are always excited if we're saddling up the horses. Sometimes we saddle up to work the cattle, but mostly, it's to head out on yet another adventure.

Saddling up with enormous energy and enthusiasm is what should happen every day of our lives. To plan your course and lead yourself to live your dreams is the greatest ride the human heart ever takes—the Greatest Adventure. It's a journey of passion and purpose, of careful thought and daily intention. And it further distinguishes those who live by design from those who live by default.

Very practically speaking, you keep pushing toward significance by pushing yourself day after day, year after year. By forming a vision and a plan for making it happen, and then following them. By mastering fundamentals and exercising strong habits that align with your purpose.

As you learn to be true to these things that make you *you*, following your internal leader happens naturally. And with time, those remote mountaintops that once seemed so impossible to reach become more than possibilities. They become realities.

YOUR FUEL

Passion is the fuel of every dream. It's what lights your inner fire and keeps it lit as you execute your plan. When you feel passionate about your vision and your future, you'll be inspired to make the journey all that it can be.

Not only does passion compel you to action, but when combined with a clear purpose, strong discipline, and reliable resources (the other topics we will cover in this final section of the book), passion puts joy in your journey. Because I want you to know that kind of joy, we will focus in this chapter on what propels your passionate pursuit. If you've been living by default for very long, you can probably pinpoint pretty quickly what has derailed you from some great adventures. Let's focus instead on what will help you—what will move you from mere goal making and vision setting, as important as they are, to actually achieving your dreams of significance. The following sections outline three elements that fuel every passionate pursuit.

1. DEFINE YOUR WHY

If you've seen the movie *City Slickers* (in my opinion, Billy Crystal at his best), you know that Billy plays Mitch Robbins, a thirty-nine-year-old husband and father who has long been living by default.

He is truly an average guy—one without a bold vision and no great system, no Master Action Plan, to back up his actions.

He has so been infected by *average* that his message to his child's grade school classroom on career day is:

Value this time in your life kids, because this is the time in your life when you still have your choices, and it goes by so fast. When you're a teenager, you think you can do anything, and you do. Your twenties are a blur. Thirties, you raise your family, you make a little money, and you think to yourself, "What happened to my twenties?" Forties, you grow a little potbelly, you grow another chin. The music starts to get too loud and one of your old girlfriends from high school becomes a grandmother. Fifties, you have a minor surgery. You'll call it a procedure, but it's a surgery. Sixties, you'll have a major surgery; the music is still loud, but it doesn't matter because you can't hear it anyway. Seventies, you and the wife retire to Fort Lauderdale, you start eating dinner at two o'clock in the afternoon, you have lunch around ten, breakfast the night before. You spend most of your time wandering around malls looking for the ultimate soft yogurt and muttering "How come the kids don't call? How come the kids don't call?" The eighties, you'll have a major stroke; you end up babbling to some Jamaican nurse who your wife can't stand but who you call mama. Any questions?

Later, talking with his wife at home, he expresses to her that he has lost his way. Wanting to help, she tells him: "Go do 'this cattle drive thing.'" She specifically tells him to take two of his buddies and that she's giving him these two weeks. Her last words are "Go find your smile."

During his time at this working cattle ranch, Mitch is challenged by a crusty old cowboy named Curly (played by Jack Palance). Curly tells him to be on the lookout for *the one thing* that makes him feel alive. That's the secret to life, he says.

Mitch does make this discovery, but not in the way he expected. While moving cattle across a river, Mitch falls in and nearly drowns. In that moment of mortality, he visualizes his children and his wife—his real *why*. And he emerges from the river a new man. He has found his smile, and he is energized for a greater future.

Returning home from his "Wild West" experience, a visibly changed Mitch greets his wife and kids at the airport. Presuming that Mitch's happier demeanor is due to the vacation from his routine, his wife suggests that he quit his job, get a fresh start vocationally. He responds, "I don't want to quit my job. I'm just going to do it better. I'm going to do everything better."

Undoubtedly, Mitch will need systems to activate and reinforce that better vision for his life. But by combining a powerful why with his newly clear View of the Summit, he is on his way toward a lifetime of great adventures, and as he says they are his "BEST days."

Interestingly, I've had the privilege of taking over seventy-five groups from our firm (over fifteen-plus years) through a weeklong training camp at our cattle ranch. Often, they have a similar break-through experience. That's mostly because they've taken time there to intentionally focus on themselves and their most amazing future, systems, strategies, and habits.

Your Greater Why

You shouldn't need an extreme vacation or a brush with death to find your why. Just take a close look at your life. As you consider what impassions you, keep these characteristics in mind:

- Your why must be bigger than you—something that stretches you.
- It has to be stronger than your desire to remain comfortable—in other words, worthy of getting off the couch and putting down your phone for.
- It needs to be greater than your greatest fear.

This last aspect is especially important. Do you know what the most common motivator in the world is? Fear. Fear is the most prevalent motivator, but love is the most powerful.

Here's how I know: Most of us wouldn't dare traverse Niagara Falls on a tightrope, not even for a million dollars. It's just too risky. The odds are probably worse than a million to one that you would fall to your death. Plus, there's that pesky fear of heights that so many of us have. Nonetheless, under different circumstances, I bet you would attempt it in a heartbeat.

Imagine you were standing on one side of the falls, and you saw your little girl hanging from the far end of that tightrope, pleading for your help. You wouldn't debate your chances of dying; you'd run for that rope as fast as you could, and you'd scoot across it however you could, and you'd doggedly keep going in spite of your fear because you'd be thinking, *I love my daughter! I have to reach her before she falls!*

The Good Book says that "perfect love casts out fear."[1] Where

there is love, fear loses its power. It may not completely exit the building, but it does lose much of its force. It takes a backseat. And in its
place comes the power and discipline we need to conquer our goals
and live our dreams.

In a far less dramatic scenario, I've seen the truth of this myself.
Our financial-services firm holds a quarterly conference called WinGS
(an acronym for "Winning in Great Strides"). During those confer-
ences, we bring together our entire organization for learning, growth,
motivation, camaraderie, and vision casting.

At one WinGS conference, I was on a panel that was taking questions from team members in the audience. Midway through, the
moderator remarked, "We have a Skype caller with a question." The
Skype figure came up on the big screen, blurry at first and then clearly
seen. It was my son Chad, calling from his room at college with a
question that had nothing to do with the topic we were on. Now I
was really confused!

"Our family has been aware of my dad's Lifetime List for many
years, and since before I was born, it's been on his bucket list to
skydive," Chad told that roomful of people. He then went on to
announce: "I'm about to turn twenty-one, and I'm challenging you,
Dad, to go skydiving with me on my birthday."

Ugh! Truthfully, I had decided long ago that I'd been delusional
when I put that on my list as a young man. Yet I was being called
out by my son, the one who, as a little guy, was horribly afraid of
heights. Over about a three-year period of time, we worked together
to help him overcome that fear, starting at Wind River Ranch family
camp one summer. They had a climbing wall that led to a zip line
that let you soar above the treetops through the mountain air. While
it seemed incredibly fun to me, it was absolutely terrifying to Chad.

Year one, Chad outright declared that he would not pursue the wall. Year two, he decided to climb the wall but didn't have great success on his own. We did get to the top together, but it was a trying, tension-filled experience for him. Year three, Chad defeated the wall and tried the zip line. His exuberance at conquering his fear of heights and flying over the treetops was still strong in my memory and had clearly left a lasting impression on him, too. Now, many years later, Chad, at almost age twenty-one, was challenging me, at age fifty, to overcome one of *my* fears and jump out of an airplane with him.

He demanded an answer in front of my entire firm. Obviously, I said yes, though it was a reluctant yes. I secretly hoped everyone would forget Chad's challenge, but of course, everyone in the firm (along with my entire family) held me accountable to keep that commitment.

The events of that day are riveted in my mind. We went to a place called Skydive Spaceland. We had researched the place and determined that only a few people had died while skydiving there! (Smile.) Arriving at the barnlike airplane hangar and donning really colorful jumpsuits was sort of the point of no return. The instructors took us through a step-by-step process, explaining how this skydiving thing works. All in all, it seemed pretty simple. After leaping out of a plane that would be flying several thousand feet in the sky—and while plummeting toward the earth—we'd reach down to our right hip and pull hard on a golf ball–like mechanism once the altimeter on our wrists hit a certain number. This would release the parachute and supposedly allow us to descend safely back to solid ground.

Right after class, we each signed a pretty remarkable release, which stated that if we fell to our deaths, it happened because we were stupid enough to go skydiving in the first place. Or at least that's how I remember it.

The next thing I knew, Chad and I were climbing into an airplane without a door. The plane itself seemed rather rickety to me. We had determined that Chad would go first, which didn't bother me one bit. I reasoned that if he chickened out, I could stay on the plane and console him on the way down.

In a few short minutes, we were at thirty thousand feet, and as quick as a whistle, Chad was out the door. I was comforted to know that both he and I were strapped to tandem jumpers with significant skydiving experience. I was comforted, that is, until my jump partner told me that in his years of skydiving, the primary parachute had only not opened four times!

As I frantically watched for Chad's parachute to open, my partner and I jumped out of the plane, too. As I'm sure you have realized by now, both Chad and I landed safely. It was a truly exhilarating experience—such a tremendous thing to do with my son. But also, in my mind, it was a onetime deal. I would never have to skydive again. *Whew!*

That sense of unspoken relief didn't get to stick around for long. About fifteen minutes after we were back on the ground, my middle son, Ryan, piped up and said, "Dad, if you were willing to do that with Chad, you'll have to do that with me on my twenty-first birthday, too." Soon after that, our youngest son, Cody, stated that he also would accept his brothers' challenge as a rite of passage into adulthood.

I'd love to be able to say that my fear subsided after the first dive and that I looked forward to doing it with each of my sons. Instead, I began praying that Chad's brothers would not follow through. Now, years later, as I share this story with you, I have skydived with Chad, Ryan, Cody, our "adopted" son Dale, and my leadership team from the office! And I've learned a few things from it, most importantly the lesson of overcoming fear with power, love, and discipline.

To this day, I feel extremely empowered to have overcome my anxieties for the purpose of modeling courage to the Reeter boys. My extraordinary love for my sons was a far stronger incentive than the fear of jumping out of an airplane. Certainly, it took some self-discipline to manage my emotions and follow through on this commitment. Ultimately, though, this experience of skydiving with each of my sons was priceless and one of my favorite accomplishments on my Lifetime List.

2. GO ALL IN

Involving your heart is another way to add fuel to your pursuit. Our son Cody evidently learned this at a young age. He was a quarterback in little league football, and one time, his coach screamed at one of Cody's teammates, "Get your head in the game!" There's probably never been a coach who hasn't said that to one of his players at one time or another. However, Cody took it a step further in the huddle and challenged the kid to get his heart in the game, too.

That's key. It's not enough to have your head in the game; you have to be *all* in—head *and* heart, mind *and* soul, working them together with your physical capacity to go the distance and make your dreams come true. Otherwise, you just show up at your job, at home, at your place of worship and do what you have to do—but you lack what really would have made it significant to you and to those around you.

Friends, we have to quit "clocking in" to our lives and being content with that. If you're living for the weekends—with your golf outings, 'Bama football, or hunting trips eliciting more excitement than leaving for work each day and coming home to your family each evening—that's when you know you're moving through life in your head. If you're too tired to engage in anything but "you time," you're not getting everything you can out of life, and you're not truly leading yourself.

Several years back, our consulting company took thousands of people in a top accounting firm through our program, which starts with a 120-question survey. These were highly compensated people; yet, with few exceptions, they were overworked and extremely unhappy. We'd ask them why they stayed in their job, and they'd respond, "Well, I'm making a lot of money," or, "It's prestigious."

My first response was: "There's nothing wrong with seeking money or prestige. But where I get concerned is when you are dissatisfied in that pursuit, and it prevents you from living a great vision. So, let's talk about how we can make adjustments and put you on a better path." I've had many similar conversations with college students. When I ask them, "So, why are you a business major?" for example, their response more often than not is, "Because my dad is in business," or, "Everyone knows that business majors make more money after college." It doesn't have anything to do with what their heart tells them.

So, I probe a little, nudging them to think deeper with questions such as: "Where are you going to be five years from now? And don't tell me where you'll be working. That kind of drives me nuts. I hope you want the job you really want, not the job you think you ought to want." I also ask: "Where would your heart take you in your career? You've told me where your head would take you. What would you do if you could do whatever you wanted to do, knowing you couldn't fail?"

You will have far better vision, and vastly more passion, if you are seeing your world with the eyes of your heart and not merely the eyes of your head. The eyes of your heart have a broad perspective—one that is not solely focused on you. The eyes of your heart also have 20/20 vision from here to eternity. They offer a powerful hope that can be renewed daily. And that's vital when you're pursuing great things.

To look at life with your heart is much like overlooking the horizon from high up on a mountain. The perspective you gain by taking in the world from a picturesque alpine outlook is a big part of the reason I love hiking in the high country. It's really clear from up there that this world is much bigger than me and what I see in my everyday life. It also reminds me that there's much more to me and my life than the facts, the bottom lines, the deadlines, and the data that fill my head from day to day. My problems and concerns get smaller, and the stuff that really matters—my passion, priorities, and purpose—gain prominence.

That sweeping view is important even in the day-to-day. Occasionally, Cindy and I have a discussion that might be better described as an argument. Most of the time, she's right (but don't tell her I told you that). If I see those situations through my physical eyes, the horizon ahead is less than inspiring. I might win a battle or two, but I lose the war, and our marriage suffers the damage. On the other hand, when I see our issues through the eyes of my heart—with the well-being of our relationship in view—I focus less on the ground where I'm standing because I'm mindful of the significance of what's ahead: our life together, long-term. Truly, after thirty-plus years of marriage, I can hardly remember the topic of any of these conversations. What we were arguing over was trivial. Cindy's value and place in my life is of far greater significance than winning any short-lived argument.

There are no ifs, ands, or buts about it: you have to lead yourself from the heart. Maybe Helen Keller was thinking something along these lines when she said, "The best and most beautiful things in the world cannot be seen nor even touched, but…felt in the heart."[2] This world-changing author, activist, and lecturer spent her entire life without physical sight or hearing, yet she recognized what many people miss: that to have no vision is a far worse condition.

The vision of the heart is starkly different and more complete than the vision of the intellect (our heads). The contrast is similar to the difference between knowledge and wisdom. The person who solely engages his intellect can accomplish good things. He or she may be able to move from survival to success on sheer aptitude alone. Bring the wisdom, though, and everything changes. Apply the heart, and miracles happen. Exponentially more gets accomplished. You reach significance, not just success.

Being all in—head and heart—will move you to another place altogether. So, get in the habit of taking a step back and seeing the big picture at heart level. It will help you discern your passion. From there, it's much easier to figure out how to pursue it.

I was blessed to serve on the Baylor University Board of Regents for nine years. In my comments at my final board meeting, I spoke of the power of combining passion and intellect in our pursuits: "Baylor is pursuing topflight, R1 research [a Carnegie Classification of Institutions of Higher Education for research activity] and world-changing outcomes. It can, and in my opinion, will, succeed. It will happen because Baylor researchers and leaders seek wisdom along with knowledge, seeing with their hearts as well as their heads."

3. SEEK FIRST TO SERVE

A few years ago, I was asked to offer a few comments on leadership at the George H. W. Bush Presidential Library and Museum at Texas A&M University. The library board, including my friend Drayton McLane, would be in attendance. That was pressure enough! Yet a few minutes before I stepped to the podium, someone commented that former President Bush himself and his remarkable wife, Barbara, were also in the audience. That rattled me a little. I mean, who was I to speak about leadership to one of the greatest leaders of our time and his wife (whom I also put in that category)?

That morning, I quoted President Bush as having said, "There can be no definition of a life of success that does not include service to your fellow man." After the ceremony, the speechwriter, who years prior had helped the president prepare the speech I'd cited, explained to me that I was mistaken in my quote. What was President Bush's reaction? Sitting there in his wheelchair, he chuckled and kidded his friend: "I think he said it better than you wrote it!"[3]

My takeaway was the extraordinary humility this world leader had exhibited toward a knucklehead like me. A prideful person would have derided me for misquoting him. Former President Bush was not that kind of man. I had several touch points with him over the years, including the opportunity to help him and his writer develop his speech for one of Northwestern Mutual's annual meetings, and he was as gracious all those other times as he was on that day at A&M.

One timeless sentiment that I always come back to is: "Whoever wants to be the greatest of all must be a servant of all."[4] By serving others before self, we add power to our lives. Serving others is a heart thing, not so much a head thing.

We humans tend to categorize our life's journey, and especially the vocational pursuit, differently than eternity does. Our title or salary are of least concern compared to whether we're serving others. Seeking first to serve, love, and care for people, and be a catalyst in their lives, is always the place to start. If you do that, other things—such as the money and the job promotions—often fall into place.

For most people, money is their starting point. Rather than producing the impetus they intend, however, this priority unknowingly produces fear and anxiety. The freedom and abundance that characterize the passionate pursuit fall away, and the journey becomes a burden.

The priority of service is something we try very hard to impress upon our new associates at Northwestern Mutual from day one. Each of them is offered a personal life coach to help him or her create a Master Action Plan. Probably the greatest thing we do differently is to focus our team members on impact as their primary driver. "Choose to impact over income," we say. "Don't blindly follow the money; tend to the entire trajectory of the journey you're on. Your path is about far more than your financial success." In other words, we tell them: Strive for significance. Make service your priority. Focus on serving others over serving yourself.

You see the difference as soon as they start in on the work. In our financial-services firm, we ask new advisers to dial the phone forty times a day. It's really hard. You can't sustain that day after day without servanthood and mission in view. It's the difference between "I'm calling forty people today because I'm concerned about them and their well-being," and "I'm calling forty people today because that's my quota."

If the latter is your concern, you'll have a tough time with people telling you no (and sometimes in an unpleasant manner). But if your priority is impact, you'll be able to keep at it, knowing that for every several rejections, you're that much closer to the person who *will* hear you out—and whose life you may be able to vastly improve.

You may recall Abraham Maslow's hierarchy of needs. Regardless of your opinion of Maslow, much can be learned from his pyramid, which pictures his theory of motivation. The bottom layer represents the most primitive of human needs, such as food and water, oxygen and sleep; each successive layer represents another, increasingly complex category of focus. As one's needs are met at each level, according to Maslow, a person progresses toward self-actualization at the tip of the pyramid, which is essentially defined as the full realization of one's potential. His apex is self-actualization, while I consider serving others to be the pinnacle—what I would call "selfless-actualization," where we are not only fully living out who we are but intentionally investing in others. Service is, I believe, the abundant, passionate pursuit that leads to significance.

DISCOVERING MY OWN PASSIONATE PURSUIT

I can verify the effect of the three parts of the passionate pursuit because of my experiences just out of college. Interviewing for my first career job was quite a process. Among other possibilities, I met with a bank and with a dynamic gentleman named Pat Murphy at Northwestern Mutual. Truthfully, I took the meeting with Pat only to gain some interview practice. Northwestern was a straight-commission job in Dallas, where I had no connections whatsoever. Compared to the other, salary-based opportunities out there, it just didn't stack up well financially. I also talked with Joe White about a position with his Kanakuk Kamps, but strangely, I did not feel called to be there.

At the top of my list was Marion Merrell Dow, a pharmaceutical company where my father had worked for many years until he retired. Ron Melton, a close friend of my dad's, was the point person for new hires, and what MMD was offering was extremely exciting: a significant base salary with benefits, plus an opportunity for commission and bonuses, plus a company car and stock options. Though I told Mr. Melton that I wanted to prayerfully consider their job offer, I felt sure I would accept it. As I prayed and pondered, though, it didn't seem like the right choice for me.

Calling him to decline was a piece of cake compared to informing my mom and dad that I had decided to join Northwestern Mutual instead. Sheer logic said that I was passing up a sure future. The position at Northwestern truly scared me. To be on straight commission would require enormous discipline. But I was trying to listen to my heart even more, and my heart said that the team at Northwestern Mutual seemed like the kind of people I wanted influencing me. I remember thinking, *If my life looks a lot like those of Pat Murphy, Al Angell, and these folks ten years from now, I will accomplish more than I'm foreseeing for myself right now.* At the same time, my gut was saying that if I could spend my days asking important questions in order to help individuals and families bring their financial and other visions to life, it could truly be a career of impact. So, I chose Northwestern Mutual and rented a pretty pricey apartment in the Village, a complex on Dallas's east end, with two fraternity brothers from college. They both had real jobs where their employer gave them a paycheck every two weeks. I got paid only if I sold things.

I didn't always sell things!

Back then, the company's systems for training were markedly different from their extraordinary systems today. I began in 1984, and I read my training. They called it *The Essentials*—a forty-hour self-study that consisted of reading each chapter and taking a test on that material. The book gave us language to memorize, and I remember it to this day. I would literally start my approach to potential clients with these words: "What I do is what we call long-term planning for the correlation of assets…" Later I would tell them, "In this time of confiscatory taxation, we've found that people, such as yourself, are interested in tax-advantaged vehicles that allow them to systematically set aside dollars for their family's financial future."

As a twenty-two-year-old who looked to be about seventeen, this approach of rote memorization was less than effective, to say the least (not to mention the impersonal nature of reciting a script). Then there was the problem of my lack of a natural market. I simply didn't know anybody in Dallas, so I resorted to calling on my Kanakuk campers and asking them to refer me to their parents!

As you can imagine, my level of productivity was far below what my bosses were expecting, and paying rent soon became a challenge. I lived on peanut butter sandwiches as a way to save money. Meanwhile, the air conditioner in my car went out. The cost to fix it was less than four hundred dollars, but I couldn't afford it. And though Cindy, whom I was dating at the time, repeatedly offered her car while she spent the summer in Europe with her family, I pridefully refused. One time, she even added that her father had said it was not good for the car to be sitting so long undriven. Still, I drove to my appointments in the sweltering Texas heat in a suit and tie. Soaked with sweat, I would literally towel off before entering the offices of my prospects. Of course, this didn't help my struggling financial-services practice, either! It felt like pure survival.

One evening toward the end of the summer, Cindy called, and I requested her prayers for the next day. I had a closing meeting scheduled with a gentleman in the Las Colinas area of a Dallas suburb, and doing business with him would mean the difference between paying rent and not paying rent. I also admitted to Cindy, "If he doesn't buy, I don't know what I'll do."

Cindy pleaded with me to take her car so that I could show up to that appointment fresh. I finally, reluctantly, agreed. The next day, on my way to the meeting, I rear-ended an oil field service truck that had stopped suddenly in the middle of the road. In those days before cell phones, I had no way of getting to a phone to inform my client what had happened, which meant I stood him up *and* wrecked Cindy's car.

I sobbed uncontrollably on the phone that night when I told Cindy what I had done. I wept again the next night after finding out from her father that the deductible on his insurance was a thousand dollars. He was so gracious to me about the wreck, telling me, "It's just a car, Jeff. It's not a big deal." But I was determined to cover the cost and get the car fixed. I just didn't know how I would come up with a thousand dollars.

Then, James Heatherington, who chaired the board of a ministry for which I volunteered, called me. "I heard about the wreck," he said, "and I want to recommend a body shop." I vividly remember the meeting with Bill Harvey, the owner. He was so kind and gracious. James had called ahead to tell him about my work with kids in the ministry. Mr. Harvey told me he would consider it a privilege to fix the car and that he thought he could potentially save me from paying at least part of the deductible. At the back of his shop, I noticed several cars with the same paint color. Mr. Harvey remarked that a couple of years prior, he'd landed the account for the City of Dallas. I asked him, "Would you be willing to discuss your financial strategies with me at some point in the future?"

"Would I be willing to?" he echoed, a little surprised. "Most financial people don't want to work with somebody in the auto body business." I assured him that it would be *my* privilege, and we set an appointment.

Bill Harvey became a wonderful friend and a great client. Meanwhile, the businessman I stood up in Las Colinas did not return my call after two attempts. I was certain I had blown that relationship. On my third try, though, we connected, and to my surprise, he apologized for being too tied up to take my previous calls. When I told him what had happened on the day of our meeting, he graciously said, "I'm still eager to get together." And when we met, he actually bought more than the amount on my "case open" sheet.

Things were starting to look up, but I was still in crisis. Soon thereafter, I received a letter from Joe White that only stirred the pot:

> Dear Jeff:
> We missed you like crazy when you left camp…
>
> How's work? I hope it's terrible so that you come to your senses and get back here with kids where you belong. God is just around the corner, Jeff, and he wants to grow mighty and big and real in your life.

At first, that letter really angered me. Upon second thought, I reasoned, *Maybe this is a job offer—and my escape route. I could quit Northwestern and work a stable job with Kanakuk that I know I would love*. Then, I thought about it further and realized that I was in this difficult spot because I'd done what I had told Joe I would never do: I'd stopped pursuing impact.

Knowing my heart for serving others, he had challenged me to boldly continue that passionate pursuit in my career. He had questioned whether I would lose sight of my heartfelt vision for people. I adamantly stated that I would not—and within weeks of joining Northwestern Mutual, I did. Though I'd joined Northwestern for the right reasons, I'd left my heart behind and lost sight of my why, all in pursuit of a paycheck.

This was the turning point. Rather than quitting Northwestern and begging Joe for a job, I decided I should first do what I told Joe I would do. So, I scrapped my scripted language and began speaking from my heart. I started going into the marketplace and explaining to people that my ultimate desire was to make a long-term difference in their lives, that I wanted to help them create a financial strategy but also challenge them to run after life more intentionally. (I said nothing about confiscatory taxation!) It wasn't as eloquent as my previous verbiage, but it was real. And because it was authentic and authentically motivated, it had power.

I specifically remember thinking that though this change would cause me to make less money (if that were possible), it would allow me to have impact and, most importantly, stay true to my heart. What a difference this made! People responded very differently to me. They experienced me as a genuine, caring person, instead of a young man citing impressive, memorized words. And my financial-services practice started to grow and grow. In time, I became a top producer in our firm and in the state of Texas, and by age thirty-four, I was given the opportunity to lead as a managing partner. I also grew to utterly enjoy what I do, so much so that I'm still at it, more than thirty-five years later.

That's what happens when you maintain the passionate pursuit. You have joy—for the long haul.

WHAT FLIPS THE SWITCH

You've probably heard the old saying: "Find your passion, and you'll never have to work a day in your life." Of course, that doesn't mean you quit working. It's more likely that, once you find your passion, you'll work harder than you've ever worked. The difference is, you'll sincerely love what you're doing—love it so much that it no longer feels like work, but fun. This can happen in your marriage, your relationship with your kids, your community service, your worship, and so on, as surely as it can happen in your job. So, saddle up, find your passion—what flips that switch in your heart—and pursue it with all your heart, soul, mind, and strength. When you do, you'll find your joy.

Lewis and Clark didn't know what they would find as they blazed new trails into uncharted territory, and neither do you. But there is so much to be said for passionately pursuing the uncommon adventures that have been earmarked for you. To live that way makes even those times when you're not exactly sure of where you're headed different. It:

- reveals your purpose in this world;
- empowers you to achieve your goals and live a life you love;
- sets you in position to multiply your impact; and

- enables you to leave a legacy for your loved ones that you—and they—can be proud of.

If this book can guide you in doing some of those things, bringing you to places where you're thriving, your aspirations are in full view, your individual abilities are fully engaged, you're meaningfully connecting with others, and you're not just succeeding by earthly standards but making an eternal impact, then I will have fulfilled my purpose in writing it.

But you have to be willing to get in the saddle and ride after this great adventure. Go make it happen. Most people aren't doing it. They won't be doing it. And certainly not in the way that you'll be doing it. They want to live their dream life and realize their passions, but they're not so interested in planning the course and following it with a daily routine. If you will, though, you'll see it happen—especially as you combine your passion with your purpose, the topic of the next chapter.

CHAPTER 10

―――――――

LIFE ON PURPOSE

There's another moment from the movie *City Slickers* that is poignant. When asked what his best day ever was, beyond the birth of his children, Mitch (Billy Crystal) tells his buddies it was the first time he went to Yankee Stadium with his dad. Until that day, Mitch had only ever seen the games in black and white on their family TV. He describes attending the game in person as being the first Yankees game he ever saw *in color*.

That's a good description of the passionate pursuit: you start to live life in full color. Add to it an understanding of your purpose, and suddenly you're operating with the clarity of a high-definition TV. The two go hand in hand, making for an optimal, unforgettable experience.

Undoubtedly, passion is a fantastic thing to have. But unless you can channel it, you're likely to scatter your energies in a hundred directions. Knowing your life's purpose provides that fixed point that you need to live on purpose. It is your true north, always directing you toward the truth of who you are and your very own summits of significance.

In case you're unclear about your reason for being placed on the planet, I invite you to imagine yourself sitting under a tree as you pause and reflect. I'm specifically thinking of Victor's Tree, a giant, three-hundred-plus-year-old oak named after my dad that's at our family ranch outside of Houston. It has an extensive canopy with roots that run as deep as the tree runs tall. (That's an apt goal for our lives, too, isn't it?) Countless folks have sat under it over the centuries, contemplating who they are and what they want their life to stand for. Why not rest awhile under its shade and consider what you're called to? The answer is already written on your heart; just look for it.

SIGNS OF YOUR DESIGN

I understand that trying to answer that "Why am I here?" question can seem overwhelming. But it's worth exploring for the confidence and clarity it will give you on the rest of your journey. Wrapped up in your purpose are all the things you're learning about yourself through this book, as well as all the dreams you will ever have and all the adventures you will ever pursue. Every calling in every season of life will flow from your purpose. It is a river that supplies every tributary of your life.

As an early step in defining purpose, we ask people who attend training sessions at the ranch, "What are your strengths, and what are your values?" This exercise is helpful. We're each born with a purpose, and its markers are on display from a young age.

What are some other markers? You discern your purpose by:

- paying attention to what your life is teaching you and has taught you;
- exploring the realities of who you are;
- identifying what you've been equipped and called to do; and
- defining significance for yourself.

Then, you find the overarching theme that connects them all.

Someone has said it so simply but so well: "One of the greatest gifts you can give the planet is figuring out what you have to offer the world and then giv[ing] it away over and over."[1] Your purpose entails what you really want out of life for yourself, but it's more than that. What *enduring change* for the better are you seeking in your family, your neighborhood, and the world at large? In other words, how do you want to be remembered? This will tell you a lot. With that answer in mind, reflect on how your uniqueness has equipped you to be that agent of change. Where are the "signs of your design" pointing you? Road signs are there for a reason: to point us to our destination. Have you figured out which destinations of significance your design is pointing you toward?

In the discernment process, you're going to naturally notice your most obvious traits and gifts, but don't make the mistake of overlooking the little things that make you *you*. Are you thinking that quirk in your personality has no meaning? Or that what others have labeled a weakness of yours is something to be embarrassed about? Were you bullied for being different? Instead of trying to distance yourself from those things so you don't stand out from the crowd, figure out how to turn them into a platform for improvement. Use them! For good! To make someone else's life better! Turn what others have perceived as a handicap into a hand of help and hope that you extend to others.

There is simply no such thing as "worthless" on this great adventure. As long as you're leading yourself, nothing goes to waste—not even those things that perhaps others made fun of growing up. They're not mistakes or garbage; they're glimmers of gold! Someday, some way, those uncommon qualities, those unusual experiences, will prove to be your currency; somehow, those quirks of yours will be your ticket to the next level in your areas of pursuit.

When you live by design, you understand that everything matters; everything has a purpose. Each uniqueness is pointing you toward the peaks you're supposed to reach during the course of your life. Each idiosyncrasy is another tool at your disposal that can keep you advancing toward your dreams. If you're on the lookout, it's only a matter of time until the significance of each uniqueness becomes apparent. Your deep-down desires, combined with your talents and personality and experiences, are the means to many uncommon adventures and exceptional experiences.

Keep leading yourself and you will see.

YOU HAVE EVERYTHING YOU NEED

I can't say what your purpose is, but I know this much for sure: when you embrace a purpose greater than yourself and selfish pursuits, things seem to fall into place. Maybe you haven't given your gifts much thought, but:

- you were born with the right *equipment*—the personality and passions, the talent and the smarts—to walk your particular trail;

- you have *traveling companions* who can help you on your way;
- every experience now and in your past has been *training* for what lies ahead;
- as you build on your opportunities and potential, you will stockpile additional *skills and disciplines* that you'll draw on in time, as you need them; and
- you have two *navigational tools*: the integrity compass and a MAP, both of which, when put to use, will allow you to plan your course and live your dreams.

Use these gifts and guides well, and you will end up in some amazing places. Places that no one has ever been before. Only be patient, and don't get ahead of your heart. It is as critical in discerning your purpose as it is in pursuing your passions.

1. Integrity Compass: Picture a compass that adds clarity to direction. It adds clarity in all aspects of your BEST life (i.e., family, fitness, relationships, faith). Within the compass itself are things like your values and your mission statement. One of my favorite things in my integrity compass is my "I Believe" page that I've been working on for decades.

2. Master Action Plan (MAP): As we've discussed previously, your MAP consists of your short-term action steps (in the various areas of your life) that can be seen against the backdrop of your longer-term vision.

THE WAY OF THE HEART

The route to success tends to be rather formulaic. Think MapQuest—enter all the right data, wait a few seconds, and *voilà*...specific directions to your destination in the minimum amount of time. With that being the case, I can see why so many thought leaders focus on success rather than significance. It's fast. It's a clean in and out. There's a quick payoff. Done.

However, we are striving for significance. Which means trying to follow the heart. And though this process does need our heads, though it does use facts and data as coordinates, that true north inside of you—the truth of who you are and what you've been called to—is more fluid than fixed. It's spiritual. It takes you on an intuitive journey in which you have to pore over your MAP, heed your compass, and take note of what your instincts are telling you more than the splashy billboards that are promoting success. The billboards will bring you to Disneyland; heeding your internal markers will bring you to the promised land.

Simply put, the heart takes longer to discern. And not everyone wants to wait for it. I think that's why a lot of the successful forty- to fifty-year-olds I talk to are frustrated in spite of their ample bank accounts and achievements. They were taught to climb the ladder of success as quickly as possible; meanwhile, their purpose—and the significance that comes with knowing it—eludes them. It was never on their radar.

Don't let that happen to you. Don't let your desire for quick money or a fast promotion keep you from your destiny. You may be tempted to abide by your watch and your speedometer, but remember: while they will bring you to a lot of cool destinations, it's your destiny that will fulfill you. Your heart aids your vision, increasing your ability to see not only more broadly (as we talked about in the previous chapter), but far more deeply, to what is timeless and priceless. It searches out not just your purpose, but all the ways your purpose can serve others.

So, when it comes to discerning your purpose, take your time. There are certain things you simply won't see until you look with your heart.

SHOW ME THE WAY

Maybe another way to say all of this is: "If you seek your way, you will find your way." Be diligent about leading yourself by all the means you can, and the way before you will open up; you will arrive where you're supposed to be.

Isn't that cool? Our dreams and our destiny intersect when we're seeking the path we are meant to take. As we live by design, we begin to notice providential signposts directing us along the way. Our destiny comes into view, step-by-step. We learn who we are, where we're going, who we were created to be, and what we need to do to make our dreams happen. And the longer we follow our singular path, the further we will go. Even more, we find joy and satisfaction in the adventure. In fact, following the path we were meant to take leads to a life of love, joy, and peace. That's exactly what happened to me at a time when I least expected it.

TO GO OR STAY?

It was the fall of 1995, and as the number two guy—the assistant managing partner—in the Dallas office of the Northwestern Mutual financial network, I had been asked to speak in Lake Geneva, Wisconsin, at a seminar for key leaders in the company. I would be giving my talk to managing partners (MPs) and their team members as well as several Northwestern executives.

That week, the group buzz was about who the home office in Milwaukee would pick to lead our prominent downtown Chicago office, now that Chicago's esteemed MP was transferring to Milwaukee. I knew about the opening; for some time, some of the company leaders in Wisconsin had suggested I put my name in the hat.

"I'm really prayerfully considering it," was my reply.

"What's to consider? Chicago is the number one office in our system!" they said. "You'd be crazy if you don't at least put your name in."

As I weighed the options for myself and my family, I knew we would land on a vision for the future, but I was unsure about where *exactly* we should go. I felt a little like ancient Israel's leader Moses as he and the Israelites prepared to exit Egypt for an unknown but promised land of peace and abundance. Moses, recognizing the vulnerability of their situation and his own human limitations, was only willing to risk the trip if he could count on God's presence with them for the entire journey. One prayer of his at that time expressed my own desire: "Now therefore, I pray thee, if I have found grace in thy sight, [show] me now thy way."[2] Then he essentially reiterated to the Lord, "But if you don't intend to go with us, then please don't move us from this place."[3]

My wife, Cindy, and I were praying for God's best for our family, which included two growing boys (and one on the way). Our attitude was: If God is at work here, we will do His will. If not, we will gladly stay put, as we loved our home and life in Dallas.

A MORNING MESSAGE

On the afternoon of September 30—the night before our seminar session—Denny Tamcsin, the head of Northwestern's field force, and I spent over two hours discussing the Chicago opportunity. From my perspective, it was the best managing partner position Northwestern had ever offered anyone. I was honored that I was even a candidate.

Denny and I had always had a special relationship. A few years earlier, under his leadership, I'd gone through a rigorous yet extremely positive Career Analysis Procedure (CAP) at the home office. This assessment process had gone so well, in fact, that Denny told Cindy and me in his office afterward, "I don't have the authority to name my successor, but if you and Cindy were willing to move to Milwaukee, Jeff, I'd love to mentor you and recommend you for the position." Though Cindy and I had prayerfully decided not to move to Milwaukee at that time, the CAP process had launched us into a more concentrated pursuit of God's master plan for our family.

The morning of my seminar talk, I awakened early for some quiet time and a run amid the beauty of Lake Geneva's autumn colors. Though I was surrounded by a magnificent display of red, yellow, and orange in the trees lining the lake, my mind was on my uncle Lowell, who was on his deathbed after an extended illness. I had made arrangements to fly to Illinois right after the session to be with him, but word had just come that he might not make it through the day. I prayed that he would hang on long enough for me to see him one last time.

During the run, my mind played one memorable scene after another, like a movie...

Memories of the summers I'd spent with him and my aunt as a child.

How fervently they had always prayed for my brother, sister, and me since they had no children of their own.

The letter of commitment I'd sent them, vowing that the values they and my parents had modeled would live beyond them.

Scattered among those memories were concerns about the future—my career path and my family's well-being, visions of what might be next, my own determination to lead myself and my family, my longing to leave a powerful legacy, prayers for mercy and wisdom in whatever was to come.

It was a sobering run, but the crisp fall air helped clear my mind and lungs and ready me for my day. As I finished, I stopped and watched a gaggle of geese on the edges of the lake. One of them took off from the group and soared into the sky, seemingly leading himself toward a determined future.

Inspired, I challenged the audience in my talk later that morning to live by design and lead themselves, the way Uncle Lowell had done, the way that lone goose had done. I then hopped a plane to Illinois.

INTO THE WOODS

When I arrived in Centralia, I took over the night shift for my aunt and my brother, and saw firsthand what a struggle my uncle had endured. It was clear he would not survive; still, I wanted him to be as comfortable as possible.

For the next few nights I stayed near him, praying, singing, reading Scripture to him—and crying. I thought of him and my aunt kneeling by their couch every evening to pray for me and my future over the past thirty-three years, and I got a greater sense of my destiny. This also gave me a stronger desire to understand how to better lead myself and my family toward God's specific plan, so I didn't miss what I—and we, as Team Reeter—was supposed to do.

Upon returning to the house after one of those nights at the hospital, the phone rang. It was Denny. He had cared enough to somehow find my aunt and uncle's number and call me personally about his decision regarding the Chicago opportunity. I wasn't the company's first choice.

I knew in my gut it was the right decision. Once we got off the phone, I put on my athletic gear and went for a run. I just had too much on my mind to go to sleep.

I started out toward the hospital, where my uncle was struggling, and then I headed to a large park that my aunt and uncle had taken us to as kids. The farther I ran, the more surprised I was at my energy level—I wasn't tired after being up all night. It seemed that the phone call had freed my vision for the future, almost as if there was now nothing blocking my view. The optimism I felt was invigorating.

After some distance, I came to the outdoor spot the locals call the Chapel in the Woods. A stone altar had been built there many years before, and I took a few moments to kneel and pray: "Now, Lord, if I have found favor in Your sight, show me thy way." Then, almost as if I was in a Robert Frost poem, I noticed a path leading into the woods behind the altar and decided to take it.

Just inside the canopy of trees, I spied a mysterious white line on the ground. *Where did this come from? Am I dreaming?* It looked like a chalk line, but why would a chalk line be here, in the middle of nowhere? Curious, I made up my mind to follow it and see where it might lead.

Into the woods it went—up hills and down, between trees and around fallen trunks, in and out of dense growth and bushes. Sometimes the foliage was so thick, I could barely see the line even a few steps ahead. Still, I ran on, my heart rate quickening as I was drawn deeper into this solitary pursuit of something I wasn't even sure was real.

At one point, concerned that I could be heading nowhere and might get lost, I left the line to take what appeared to be a shortcut out of the woods. But within moments, I was surrounded by thorns and briars. The farther away from the path I went, the thicker the briars and the deeper the scratches on my legs and arms. To retrace my steps would cause more nicks and cuts. Yet I made the painful decision to return to the white-line path, realizing it was my best option.

Through the trees I continued, brushing past limbs, the crunch of fallen leaves and snapping twigs underfoot, my pace as measured as I could keep it on the uncertain trail. Soon the white line led to the lip of the creek—and didn't stop. It picked up again on the other side.

Where did *this line come from, that it could jump water like this?* I wasn't sure what was going on, but after experiencing the consequences of my previous detour, I wasn't about to leave the line again if I could help it. Yet the creek was too wide for me to jump, and the water was running too cold for comfort. *What should I do?*

It was then that I spied a rock in the middle of the current. I wasn't sure I could make it across on just that one bit of footing. Maybe, though, it was possible with a running start and some faith.

Sure enough, it was.

Now safely on the other side, I kept running. Then, up on the right, nestled on the edge of the park, I spied a white house with shutters, with a street in front of it. *Civilization!* I thought. Seeing that it was a true shortcut to the road I'd been on before entering the park, I diverted from the white line again.

As I ran along the edge of the property, I suddenly heard something coming at me, growling. Back to the white line I turned, my adrenaline surging, just as the Doberman's chain reached its end. From there, I followed the line undaunted—out of the woods, into a wide-open meadow, and finally to the gated entrance of the park, where the line ended. That's when I noticed what I had never noticed as a kid: its name was Joy Park. The sign nearby said it was dedicated in 1946. My uncle would've been thirty-four years old at that time.

In the early-evening hours of October 2, 1995, my uncle Lowell passed away.

On October 5, 1995, my thirty-fourth birthday, I shared the goose story at my uncle's funeral.

Two months later, the home office contacted me again: "We have the managing partner position in Fort Worth coming available, but we know you probably wouldn't want to go there…"

Actually, I *was* interested. It was underperforming, the reps were undermotivated, and it had fallen toward the bottom of the charts in the Northwestern system. Yet this office was full of great people with strong potential. To me, something about it sounded appealing. Sounded like a calling. Sounded like our future. Enough so that on February 1, 1996, I became managing partner at Northwestern Mutual in Fort Worth.

I could've run after success off the white line, pleading for the top office and seeking to make a name for myself. Instead, because I knew that my destiny wasn't just success but significance, I made the decision according to my purpose and chose the place where I could best serve and help others in their journeys.

The crazy white-line experience gave me a vivid word picture. It felt like a line put there for me specifically. When I got off it, things didn't go well. My run on the line started with prayer in the chapel in the woods. It was a run of success, but, more importantly, it was a run of significance.

YOUR LINE AND MINE

I learned soon after my run through Joy Park that the white line was indeed a chalk line, put in place for a cross-country meet scheduled for later that weekend. Nevertheless, I considered it providential, because it gave me a lasting picture of a life by design.

In retrospect, I can see that the chalk line at Joy Park was symbolic of the path I was seeking to be on. Hoping not to let circumstances deter my steps (at least not for long); not letting other people choose my route. Taking inventory of my strengths and each year creating a Master Action Plan. Seeking to establish a vision for how I wanted to live. Taking specific, well-timed steps to reach my goals, and seeking to practice the daily and weekly disciplines that would get me there. In other words, I was trying hard to run the unique path designed for me, as I followed my purpose with both my heart and my mind to the next destination, believing it would deliver me to a place of joy and satisfaction.

Now, you're probably thinking, *I could lead myself, too, Jeff, if only I had a white line to follow!* True. But let me challenge you, because you do have a white line, a path you're meant to take—only with faith it's inside of you rather than in front of you. You won't necessarily know the specifics at every turn; there will be blind curves and obstacles that crop up. But the path is far more evident once you're leading yourself. Take the apparent shortcut, the route that looks easiest, and you may enjoy success, but you won't reach your destiny. Set a plan, however, that aligns with your purpose, and suddenly your own white line becomes more apparent.

This is an important principle: keep as close to the line as you can. Not only is it your route to adventure and joy, but everything about your life—your desires, your dreams, your goals, your direction, and how they all filter into your destiny—is more evident when you're near the line.

You may not yet have found your purpose, but you simply won't know what you were put on this earth for as long as you're over in the hedges, doing nothing to identify it. On the other hand, the more you seek the way, the more the path in front of you will unfold. If you'll do what you are learning to do in this book, it will appear. You may not be able to see it with your mind, but it becomes apparent by looking with your heart.

Ironically, as you lead yourself, you will be led. Not just providentially by a higher power, but by your specific design. You'll come to see that all the things that make you *you*—not just your talents and interests and personality but even your dreams, your past, and your pain—are like signposts, showing you where to go next and how to become who you were meant to be. Read the signs and follow your line.

My life experience has convinced me that Something, Someone vastly greater than myself is operating behind the scenes of my life. At the main office for our financial-services firm in Houston, we have several conference rooms. Several years back, I was asked to name those rooms. I sought to assign words that would be meaningful to our clients, our financial advisers, and our entire corporate team.

Three of those boardrooms are named Legacy, Destiny, and Providence. The legacy we have been handed down from our predecessors is foundational to our destiny, as is the lasting legacy we will pass along, with the help of Providence, to those who succeed us.

Often, because we fail to grasp that sense of eternal timing, we may not see Providence at work in the links between legacy and destiny. Nevertheless, a divine hand is always guiding us and our circumstances as we pursue the uncommon adventures of our life's journey. And so, as we lead ourselves, we not only start to lead others who are looking to us for guidance and direction toward their own summits, but we also find that *we* are being led. And that assurance is what allows us to complete our race with excellence.

Leading yourself, choosing to do life differently, doesn't guarantee that you'll be certain about every detail of your journey—yet you stay the course regardless. This was an important thing for me to grasp. Remain true to who you are, abiding in what you've been purposed to do, and you'll end up time and again absorbed in the joy, fulfillment, impact, and influence that come with the territory of significance.

Trust your heart, not just your smarts. Pursue impact over income, letting love be your motivator instead of fear. Choose realistic optimism, never pessimism. Decide how to become your best you versus letting somebody else decide for you—and then devise a plan to make that happen that fits your design. As you do, it's almost as if your purpose finds you.

CHAPTER 11

THE HABITS OF SIGNIFICANCE

To plan your course and live your dreams, you certainly need all the big-picture elements we've talked about: an understanding of where you are and where you've been, a view of where you're going that includes a Master Action Plan, plenty of passion to fuel your journey, and a well-defined purpose to focus you. Once those elements are in place, it's time to develop an Immediate Action Plan that executes your long-term vision, and then draft a Daily Action Plan for each summit you're pursuing. For when it comes to executing such a bold vision, the doing is in the details—you have to lead yourself to do what is required of you day by day and week after week, and, most essentially, install disciplines that will progressively deliver you to your dreams.

No experienced mountain climber attempts to summit a

significant mountain on the first day of a climb. Instead, he or she ascends a level at a time, in successive, well-planned stages that allow the body a chance to adjust to the altitude before making the last, big push toward the top. It's no different as you strive toward the various summits of significance in your life's journey. By taking aim in the right direction each day, following a manageable plan of action, you'll be ready—body, mind, and spirit—when it's time for the final ascent on each uncommon adventure.

DESIGNING YOUR DAILY LIFE

Designing your life around a Daily Action Plan will ensure that you live your entire life by design. As you devise your plan, one summit at a time, make sure you uphold these choices as priorities:

1. *Choose to become the best you possible.* You're not striving to be *the* best, or the G.O.A.T.—the "greatest of all time" (unless you're capable of that, of course); you're going for *your* best, and trying to consistently raise the bar on what your best is. Ask yourself: *When am I at my best? How can I replicate that in my everyday life?*

2. *Choose habits that will give you your best life.* Defaulting to bad habits takes almost no effort at all. Thankfully, choosing great habits isn't hard, either—it only looks that way from the outside. As you begin a disciplined, day-by-day pursuit of significance, you quickly realize that the habits that once seemed so needlessly painful are actually empowering. There's a freedom in strong habits. You're invigorated. They power your purpose and strengthen your

vision. They produce a flow that not only makes your whole life run more smoothly—like oil in an engine— but almost naturally moves you along to the next level.

Supposedly, it takes twenty-one days to develop a new habit. In the short term, that may feel like an eternity. But to put up with twenty-one days of discomfort to position yourself for a lifetime of what you want is not such a big deal—not when the dividends are so huge.

3. *Choose the best frame of mind.* Each of us tends to be dominated by one side of the brain or the other—either the logical, serious left brain that delays gratification for the sake of a goal, or the spontaneous, creative right brain that always wants to have fun. While both sides are essential to a life by design, they each must be kept in check to achieve our goals. (Because if there's no fun to your disciplines, you're not going to stick with any plan of action.) In the end, the dog you feed is the one that will win. But let me propose a better frame of mind that helps *you* win, not one dog or the other!

    Let's call the right brain "Thor" and the left brain "Little Guy." Thor is really strong; Little Guy is really smart.

    Little Guy has convinced you to set a daily goal to get up before work and go for a run. Now, suppose it's a cold winter day and your alarm has just gone off. Thor speaks up instantly: "Stay in bed. Don't worry about exercising today. Hit the snooze." Little Guy says, in a squeaky voice, "Get up! We have goals. We want to make something of ourselves. This is an important day."

    Rather than feeding only one dog and making them

fight, get both of them working in tandem toward the same end. The next day, try setting the alarm next to your bed for the time you want to get up to run. Set a second alarm with a loud buzzer, next to your kid's bed, to go off five minutes after your alarm. That way, you'll have to get up at the first alarm, because if the second one goes off, your spouse is going to kill you.

I did this for a number of years: I would get up, go kiss the baby, and then go for a run. Getting up and exercising made Little Guy happy; meanwhile, kissing the baby and going for a run (which is something I love to do) kept Thor satisfied as well.

Rate your *mental toughness*, your effectiveness at listening to your left-brain "Little Guy."

WEAK   STRONG
<   >
1   2   3   4   5   6   7   8   9   10

Rate your *mental agility*, your effectiveness at letting your right-brain "Thor" have fun—within limits.

WEAK   STRONG
<   >
1   2   3   4   5   6   7   8   9   10

Write down one situation where you need to get both sides of your brain working in tandem. What ideas do you have for making this happen?

THE POWER OF HABIT

You reach any summit by turning it into a series of small steps. These daily or weekly disciplines have to be meaningful yet doable. More than easy but less than impossible. A little scary, even, but not paralyzing. It sounds pretty simple—simple enough that anyone can do it. Yet people rarely put the power of habit to work in their life.

In Malcolm Gladwell's book *The Tipping Point*, we learn that successful people become successful through thousands of hours of skills training and practice. I would add to that: people who lead themselves even higher, to significance, spend day after day in the disciplined pursuit of internal growth. Their continuous pursuit of the characteristics of significance—including love, joy, peace, patience, kindness, goodness, faithfulness, gentleness, and self-control—helps them live at capacity and sustain positive energy through their daily activities. There is a Greek word, *dunamis*, that applies here. To me, it means super-abounding power, energy, strength, or ability. It is the root of our English words *dynamite*, *dynamo*, and *dynamic*. I believe *dunamis* is a spiritual strength that comes from God to people in the habit of looking to Him.

Our destination isn't about perfection; the daily pursuit is key. If you will discipline yourself to do the little things each day that defaulters seldom do, you will accumulate positive results. And in those small steps and daily choices, futures are made.

You're essentially putting compound interest to work for you. I've often challenged clients in our financial practice to set aside $100, $1,000—however much money works for their circumstances—per month for their family's financial future. Einstein called compound interest one of the great wonders of the world. In a way, it does seem almost a miracle that small, consistent deposits can exponentially become a vast fortune in a matter of time. People likewise discipline themselves in little ways day after day, understanding that sustained discipline in the right direction produces gains that multiply numerous times over.

I am grateful to have experienced, at least to some extent, the value of strong disciplines. So here are some habits that have helped me and many other people keep trekking toward our goals. You'll want to add your own take on these ideas, but these are beneficial regardless of your specific vision. It's all about making sure your life makes the kind of difference you were meant for.

THE HABIT OF…HABIT

Do you exemplify life attributes that lead to principle-centered success? In many ways, we *are* our habits. They are the spirit and mentality by which we live. For better or for worse, we're clothed in them like nuns: a bad habit restricts us and sabotages our efforts, while a positive habit produces confidence and the energy to keep going toward our goals. Sometimes we get into the habit of making poor choices. Thankfully, when the "clothing" is no longer working for us, we can switch it out for something that suits us better.

So, label your bad choices for what they are. Take responsibility for them so you don't make the same mistakes. And then exchange your bad habits for high-quality ones.

You also want to be sure to establish positive habits where you've had none at all. A good place to start is with a daily time of reflection. This is a chance to review your goals and draw up a Daily Action Plan, setting your sights on what's truly valuable in your trek toward significance. Such a focus helps you effectively prioritize your activities until the day is done.

As you go through the day, check off the boxes. I understand that not everybody likes to check boxes. For me, it helps. It's also a way to feed both Thor (who likes the quick gratification) and Little Guy (who loves that I'm making progress toward my long-term goals). Each day, I check the boxes on my Daily Action Plan, and then I grade myself at day's end in each category I care about so that I can continually improve on tomorrow's plan.

THE HABIT OF BELIEF

I can't stress enough the importance of belief, even in leading yourself on a daily basis. If someone can change their beliefs ever so slightly, they will change their behaviors little by little each day. And by changing their behaviors, the trajectory of their life changes.

I had the distinct privilege of playing college football for Grant Teaff. Coach Teaff wrote a book entitled *I Believe*. When I think back on his impact in my life as a college student, but, more importantly, his impact in my life since college, this is probably his most important lesson: Coach taught us to believe in ourselves. He taught us to have a bolder vision than we would have had without him. And possibly most importantly, he believed in *us*. His belief in me for the past thirty-two years since Baylor is more significant than his confidence in me when I was at Baylor.

I'm not going to try to articulate exactly what *belief* means for you. Maybe it's, "Believe in yourself," or, "Believe in God." What I do know is that what you believe is critical. At all costs, do not put your confidence in lies. Habitually seek and believe truth. Set your mind and heart on what is honorable, right, pure, lovely, and admirable. It's an important ingredient in an extraordinary life.

THE HABIT OF EXCELLENCE

Will Durant, the groundbreaking American historian and philosopher, once summarized some of Aristotle's thought in this way: "We are what we repeatedly do. Excellence, then, is not an act, but a habit."[1] The essence of excellence is the mastery of fundamentals—persistent execution at increasingly higher levels. One new adviser in our firm, after hearing this, told me, "This gives me hope, because anyone can get in the habit of mastering fundamentals; I don't have to pull off some incredible feat to achieve excellence."

Do you give your best, day in and day out? Do you show up on time? Do you work hard, love hard, try hard? Do you leave people, places, and things better than you found them?

One dad I know of taught his sons this habit in part by training them to put their shopping cart properly in the stall, back in line with the other carts, not leave it in the store parking lot or dumped haphazardly in the stall. My own dad wanted me to restack our woodpile as a kid. I did it by throwing the logs in another pile. He showed me how to stack the wood starting with a platform of a few logs so that the bulk of the wood wasn't sitting on the ground. His message? "A job worth doing is a job worth doing right."

Our three sons were athletes growing up. When they were young, I coached each of them in Little League Baseball. I so fondly think back on those days now...

Each of our teams had chants that we would yell over and over. "What is winning?" I'd ask. And the boys would yell back,

"Doing our best and having fun!" I would ask the team, "What are the 'eye of the tiger' principles?" The boys would scream, "Respect! Personal responsibility! Positive attitude!" We coaches wanted the boys to redefine winning. If they did their best with a smile on their faces, they would win. Maybe not that day or in that game, but in life for sure. We wanted them to take personal responsibility for themselves. If one of them struck out, it wasn't the umpire's fault. That player owned the outcome. We would respect each umpire's authority and call of the play, even if we didn't always agree with it. We could choose a positive attitude even in the negative situations.

Another thing that I loved, thinking back on it, was that if a kid hit a home run in the game or pitched really well, the coaches would ask them (and usually their parents) to stay after the game with us. We would take a moment and tell them how proud we were of them maximizing their best selves. Then, we would have them help us pick up all the trash around the stands at the ballpark and put it in the big trash can. And you know what? Those young men grew to take pride in picking up the trash!

Because you become what you repeatedly do, intentionally pursuing the habit of excellence prepares you to be a person of character and influence—a winner inside and out. People will learn that they can rely on you, and that alone will cause them to look to you as a leader and an influencer.

THE HABIT OF GOING THE EXTRA MILE

A few years ago, "Beyond" was my theme for the year. Each day, as a part of my early-morning quiet time, I reflected on what this word means. Whatever your vision is today, whatever your goals are now, plan to go even further and see where it takes you.

My dad was fifty when I was born. And though he was a lot older than my friends' dads, he went the extra mile for me all the time. This is part of his legacy to me, and it has shaped me in numerous ways. When I wanted to be a pitcher in my midteens, Dad would have me throw forty pitches to him every night. During basketball season, he would rebound for me—in his sixties! He dislocated his little toe one night while I was shooting, and he simply shifted it back into place and then said, "Ten more." As you can imagine, having a dad who outdid other dads in those little ways made me want to do the same for my kids. He also kept trying to outdo himself.

Extra work *works*. Plain and simple. And people notice. Every time you go above and beyond what's expected or what others are doing, you're a step closer to the summit. So, get in the habit of both outdoing the next guy and, more importantly, outdoing what you did yesterday. It's never trespassing to go beyond your own boundaries.

THE HABIT OF MANAGING YOUR MINUTES

Many years ago, I read Stephen Covey's *Principle-Centered Leadership*, where he talked about managing the first minute of your day so that you start off in a powerful, focused way. I felt so compelled by his words that, after hearing of a guy who got up at 4:45 a.m., I began getting up at 4:44 a.m., and I would use that first minute of the day to pray.

Prayer on my knees is still how I choose to start my day. By design, I put myself in a position where I'm reminded that I am lesser, and God is greater—a reminder that carries over into the rest of the day.

A few years after reading Covey's book, I decided it was equally important to manage the last minute of my day. I had attained a certain level of success in my life but was having trouble sleeping because what was in my brain wasn't positive or helpful. So, I made it a habit to end my day on a high note: with prayer and by reading or listening to an affirming word of truth. I found that managing what entered my mind as I was about to sleep made an enormous difference.

Saying "sweet dreams" is a nice sentiment, but what does that really mean? I'm a believer in the biblical psalm that says: "Even at night my heart instructs me."[2] We can use the last minute of today as an impetus for tomorrow's success.

I try to manage all the minutes in between as well. I tackle the hard things on my Daily Action Plan first. I also work to structure my day more holistically, so that it doesn't feel like I'm trying to ride two unicycles.

I'll confess, I'm probably a little over the top on this. I am a serial multitasker! For instance, I try to accomplish two or three things when I'm brushing my teeth. My elliptical at home is set up so that I can listen to a podcast, read a book, dictate letters or notes, or have a conference call, all while exercising.

INVESTED IN TOMORROW

Viewed from the standpoint of success, habits are valuable because they strengthen your position today. But what makes our habits so incredible is that every good habit you deposit into today is an investment in tomorrow, where it really counts. I didn't see the difference when I was younger. Now, it's more than apparent.

In my teens and early twenties, I was in the habit of working out so I would look okay at the beach. Once I married Cindy, I worked out to look good for my bride. Now I do it to sustain my vitality as a husband, a dad, a mentor, a boss, an outdoorsman, and a future granddad. The why has changed, but not the habit. And while I do still want to look good for Cindy (though that's not what's important to her), I've come to see that there's a greater end in sight.

As you accomplish the small steps that lead to every summit on your journey, you are not only making today your masterpiece, as legendary UCLA basketball coach John Wooden used to say, but you're giving yourself a gift for tomorrow. You may need to start at base camp and work your way up one step at a time, but that's okay. Every climber who has ever reached the summit of Everest has done it the exact same way.

BUILDING HABITS THAT LAST

Strategize about how to better spend your assets. Objectively step back and determine, "Based on what I want in each area of my life, what daily actions give me the best chance of reaching those summits?" You especially want to make sure you're spending your time and money in ways that are getting you closer to your goals.

Mark it and review it. Document each goal on your Immediate Action Plan, then create a Daily Action Plan each morning. In his book *Think and Grow Rich*, Napoleon Hill talks about putting a timetable to a goal and putting it all in writing. Otherwise, you're simply dreaming dreams. Dreams need a plan, a calendar, and regular review for the chance to become missions accomplished.

Start moderately. How do you move from base camp to the next level? Or from success to significance? One step at a time. If developing new habits feels daunting, try changing two things courageously, not ten. Small success breeds more success, and success breeds confidence. And confidence? It produces momentum. Momentum is what gets you up the mountain, through any obstacles, all the way to the top. What's more, one good habit begets another. Life habits motivated by great vision and fueled by specific, measurable goals keep you tracking toward your goal.

For example, let's assume you have a vision to lose forty pounds in the next year. What two steps could you take to get there? Maybe your answer is, "Eat better and exercise." Now make it more specific, so that it's measurable. What do you need to do to take a small step in that direction starting now? What if you started skipping dessert, and you get up fifteen minutes earlier tomorrow morning and make one lap around your block? To keep it focused on small steps is key. I'd rather you start out doing less and sustain it, versus trying to do too much and quitting shortly thereafter.

Are you convinced you can do more than that—perhaps walk a mile? Then go for it. Whatever step you commit to, keep moving in the direction of the summit little by little. When next week comes, set your benchmark higher. If you walked that mile in fifteen minutes, challenge yourself to do it a minute faster this coming week. And before you know it, you'll be jogging a mile without being sore the next day!

Make up your mind before you're tempted. I had a youth pastor tell me once, "You make choices when you're vertical that you're not going to get horizontal with a girl." Similarly, when I was eighteen, working at Kanakuk as a counselor, my boss Joe White would often run from the lake to the football fields to get a workout in. One day, I decided to run with him. As we were winding our way up Cardiac Hill at K2 Camp, Joe said to me, "We'll be running by the pool in a little while, so prepare your mind."

"What are you talking about?" I asked.

"There will be a bunch of girls in swimsuits when we get up there," he said. "Think about how to keep a wholesome focus before we crest the hill."

I promise, you can talk yourself out of trouble in advance much more easily than if you wait until you're face-to-face with it. It doesn't matter whether your weakness is french fries, the opposite sex, beer, fast cars, or shopping. Say no now. Prepare yourself ahead of time. Then you don't have to think about it when your thinking isn't as clear.

Skip the shortcuts. For the time it takes to establish a positive habit, it takes only a moment of weakness to break one. Our culture gives us plenty of outs and shortcuts—low-calorie versions of our favorite foods, shortened workout programs, and so on. But we need all-or-nothing thinking and behavior if our hearts are set on significance. Let's say I'm not eating sugar. Then I can't have even a bite of cake. If I'm going to run each morning before work, I can't take a day off just because I don't feel like exercising. Leading yourself means going hard and being true to yourself and your aspirations all day, every day.

CHAPTER 12

WHAT (AND WHO)
WE TAKE WITH US

As we've seen throughout this book, the journey from survival to significance is accomplished by maximizing your resources, your opportunities, and your mind-set. With your resources, you want to take great care regarding what—and whom—you take with you. Your travel gear and your traveling companions can speed your success, or virtually ensure your failure.

YOUR TRAVEL GEAR

I've learned the hard way that I'm much more likely to reach the summits I've dreamed of if I've mindfully assembled my travel gear—

the "equipment" I'll need to make my way to significance and stay the course.

I'm a little embarrassed to admit how much of an outdoor adventure gear junkie I am. I'm constantly researching the latest and greatest advances in order to enhance my outdoor experiences and further decrease my load. Often by default, hikers or climbers end up carrying things that weigh them down. Every one of us needs to not only meticulously predetermine every item we're carrying, but make sure it's essential. On an uncertain journey, carrying no extra weight is truly important.

A few years ago, I had the opportunity to climb Longs Peak in Colorado, a fourteen-thousand-foot incline, with two of our sons. Cindy and I had unsuccessfully attempted to summit the peak during our fortieth birthday year. Fifteen years later, I was at it again.

The first time I pursued the Longs Peak summit with Cindy, I didn't plan as well. By the second effort with my sons, I'd learned how to lighten my load and increase my chances for success. In preparing for this climb, I went to REI and purchased a Gregory Zulu 30 Pack, a ventilated men's hydration mountain pack. The pack can hold nearly eight gallons of water but weighs less than two and a half pounds when empty. I determined that I would need 120 ounces of water (just under a gallon) for our journey up and down the mountain. And fifteen miles later, as we returned to the trailhead where we'd started our climb, I literally took my last drink of water.

If I pack that carefully for a single day's journey to a mountain peak, how much more carefully should I scrutinize the baggage I carry with me in my adventures through life? Here are the items I consider crucial for having the best chance of reaching significance:

- a MAP
- a compass
- a Life Book

We've already discussed the need for a MAP and an integrity compass in order to live by design. In your lifetime of adventures, a MAP is critical because it helps you unpack and integrate what's important to you. It guides you in thinking through how to be systematic and intentional as you work toward your goals. Likewise, knowing how to follow your compass in pursuit of a balanced, whole-life adventure is essential because it always points you toward true north, your purpose for being on this planet. Meanwhile, your Life Book helps you execute on and implement each step of your Master Action Plan so that dreams actually see fulfillment.

In my Life Book, I do life. My Life Book is a leather-bound compilation of pages that allows me to systematize my entire journey, so I'm living in a more organized way. Even though I do journal in it, it is far more than a journal. It's full of items that I'm focusing on daily.

At the front of my Life Book I keep my MAP, which details a vision and strategy for each area of my life in the current calendar year. I love mapping out a current strategy for my relationship with Cindy and each of our sons. I love visualizing the success of our financial-services firm and the impact we might have throughout the next twelve months. In each specific area of priority, I seek to be intentional. Truthfully, it's messy but also energizing.

Beyond the current calendar year is the View of the Summit that we've talked about as well, a five-year vision of where and who I want to be. The rest of my Life Book contains page after page of synergizing quotes, thoughts, prayers, and ideas that help me stay on track. I write down strategies and goals, motivating words that come to mind, and books I want to read, along with what I learn when I do read them.

I've also included a longer-term vision timeline that helps me forecast far beyond five years. While much of it is a prognostication of probabilities, at the same time, I know the exact day and year of my thirty-fifth wedding anniversary and when I will retire from Northwestern. So, in my Life Book, I am simultaneously engaging with the current strategies of the next year, visualizing probabilities in the next sixty months, and projecting what the longer-term future might hold twenty-five years from now.

I use my Life Book to both keep me on course and help me balance my goals. This is necessary because the longer you pursue significance, the more you understand that everything in your life is connected. It doesn't work to separate your business life from your personal life, as if they're distinct segments. We need a much greater integration. My Life Book helps me sync my priorities.

As my buddy Jeff Turner says, "The balance between family and work is ever-evolving—it looks different today than when my children were little, for example." And though a perfect balance can probably never be fully achieved because life is always changing, seeking a balanced, all-encompassing life of integrity and intentionality *by design* is still worth striving for.

You might add other things to your backpack as well. Almost everywhere I go, I take along what I believe to be the best book ever written, the Bible, as well as a three-ring binder with projects that I'm working on—it's my organizing system to keep me from dropping any of the things I'm juggling. I am also constantly packing books I'm currently reading. But I'm seldom without my MAP, my integrity compass, and my Life Book.

WHAT YOU MUST LEAVE AT HOME

We've talked about many things in the previous chapters that you obviously don't want to take with you: default thinking, ineffectual habits, vices, and so on. We also have to be careful not to take the weight of past negative experiences with us. These past experiences often travel with us, along with new ones we pick up. It's as if we are carrying a backpack full of rocks on our journey. We continue to fill it, seldom unloading much.

In truth, we can never completely empty our backpacks, just as we can never truly erase our past experiences. Truly, we shouldn't want to erase the past. The goal might be to see it differently. Seeing it as a legacy can enhance our destiny. To pursue our greatest and highest life, our backpacks need to be inspected from time to time. Otherwise, our energy and resources are wasted carrying harmful things that only drag us down and keep us at base camp. We have to let certain things go if we want to have the resources and supplies to make an impact in the lives of others.

So, before you head out on your next adventure, take time to not only make sure you're bringing the things you'll need to accomplish your goal, but examine what you are carrying around that you shouldn't be. In particular, be sure to check for rocks.

That may seem an absurd suggestion, because who would ever carry rocks with them? Yet people do it all the time. I've seen people load up their backpacks with so many rocks that they can barely move. And then they wonder what's holding them back. What kind of rocks am I talking about? The rocks of unforgiveness, fear, or anger. Is there anybody you need to forgive or whose wounding you haven't dealt with appropriately?

This is one of the things we talk about at our firm's weeklong training camp for new associates. A couple of years ago, weeks after one of these training camps, I walked into a conference room back at the office in Houston, in advance of our team's Monday-morning meeting, and was surprised to find one of our associates already seated.

"I've been waiting for you," said this strapping former college tight end and now financial adviser. And then, without any further comment, he declared, "I forgave him." His face was resolute but glowing with joy.

"Who?" I asked.

Before he could answer, a surge of emotion swept over him, his shoulders heaving as he tried to control his breath. Through tears, this strong young man looked at his hands—hands that had gathered in many passes in stadiums full of Big 12 Conference fans on autumn Saturdays—and whispered, "My dad.

"I let go of the rock," he continued.

I listened intently to his heartbreaking story. His father had tragically passed away when Matt (not his real name) was a teenager. The death had left Matt's mom and family in a pretty tough spot, and he'd been angry about the hardship all these years.

What a relief it was to see the joy of his heart in the simple act of forgiveness. From that point forward, he was free—free to lead himself to the places he intended to go, free to experience every uncommon adventure to the maximum.

What's in your backpack? Any rocks? Any things that are there by default, simply because you haven't dug deep? What burdens are you carrying around that you need to leave behind? You won't be able to thrive until you've removed any excess weight from your pack.

Not only do you want to remove any rocks from your own pack

before you head for the trail, but you want to make sure you haven't left rocks in someone else's pack. Don't leave a legacy of anger or neglect in the lives of those who depend on you. As much as you can, take responsibility for where you've wronged others, apologize to them, and try to make things right so that both you and they can move forward.

YOUR TRAVELING COMPANIONS

In addition to carefully chosen travel gear, we have to decide who to invite with us in our passionate pursuit. As we pursue all the adventures we're created for over the course of our lives, perhaps the greatest reward of all is getting to share the joy and the challenges with others. Without traveling companions, our quest loses its zest.

My first try at Longs Peak made this so apparent to me. Because Longs Peak had been on my Lifetime List for years, Cindy had let me talk her into doing that hike with me for our fortieth birthdays, in spite of her fear of heights. It's really hard to reach that summit. It's not technically difficult, but highly dangerous. There are three-thousand-foot sheer drops surrounding the peak—exactly the kind of thing that doesn't help cure a fear of heights.

Nevertheless, Cindy and I trained for several months and went with friends. At one o'clock in the morning, wearing headlamps, we started on the trailhead. Cindy got through the boulder field like a champ, and we all got through the Keyhole and across the Ledges (a two-foot path with a sheer drop if you step wrong) in pretty good time. These were places we'd prepared for. But the real test of one's will comes at a crevasse between two rocks requiring a person to lunge upward and grab a peg. That's the point when Cindy declared:

"I don't care about topping Longs Peak, but I do care about raising three sons. Summiting matters to you, honey, so you go ahead and finish the climb, and I'll meet you back at the Keyhole."

I told her, "I'm not going to summit without you. This is our trip." So, we did not push for the top. We were close, but it was more important that whatever we did, we did together.

In retrospect, I probably shouldn't have persuaded Cindy to make the climb. It certainly wasn't something she dreamed of doing. Yet I appreciate her willingness to support me in this goal of mine. For her to actually risk hiking that far up the mountain with me and then to encourage me to complete the climb? My wife is the best! She helps me be my best, and she gives me her best. I couldn't ask for a better traveling companion. I've reached far more summits because of her than I ever could have without her.

When you invest in good people, and they in you, there is always a great return on investment. As you think through who you want on your climbing team, look for people who not only spur you higher but are striving high themselves—people who are committed to their own best and who seek your best.

I'm a fan of the North Face gear and their slogan: "Never stop exploring." On the company's website, it reads: "Exploration changes lives. When we search out new experiences, overcome obstacles, and connect with each other, we change ourselves."[1]

The North Face slogan reminds me of our firm, the Texas Financial Group. I'm so proud of and grateful for that group of people. Not only the advisers, but also the team of champions gathered around those advisers. We have pursued life at its BEST together for several years. We are journeying toward EXTRAordinary! None of us have been willing to admit to arriving at that significant summit, but I feel strongly that many of our folks continue to get really close! Recently, though, in an encouraging note to them, I wrote about our journey together. My statement was, "Cultural excellence is not a place to arrive at but a destination to pursue. It is sometimes difficult, even clumsy, but it's worthwhile."

LOCATION, LOCATION

On our family ranch is a beautiful meadow that runs along the banks of Four Mile Creek. Some of the trees there are spectacular. One of them, a pecan tree, has such an enormous trunk that it is in the top five in all of Texas in its circumference.

Why is that tree thriving? I'm sure its location has a lot to do with it. There's an age-old psalm that talks about trees planted near a stream of water. Those that are end up growing roots so deep that they thrive all year long, and they bear much fruit in season (Psalm 1:3).

The same could be said of us as individuals who are seeking to grow strong and bear fruit for generations to come. Our location matters. Our proximity to a water source can mean the difference between thriving and barely surviving. What waters our roots and helps us flourish are the positive, nourishing people in our lives.

Who waters your roots? Who are your go-to people who help you grow and reach higher? Who can be a catalyst for your extraordinary pursuit?

As I'm writing this, Cindy and I are about to head out to our ranch that is home to not only Victor's Tree but to those thriving, humongous trees in the meadow. We are meeting five couples out there, as we do many holiday weekends.

The Hayeses, the Harbors, the Willses, the Snows, and the Brigmans have had a huge impact in our lives for the past forty years. Where would I be without these guys? We are Baylor University Phi Gamma Delta ("FIJI") fraternity brothers—brothers from another mother!—and we live by the slogan: "FIJI. Not for college days alone." These guys hold me accountable. They keep me focused on the right path. They expect excellence of me. If I get off course, they grab me by the scruff of the neck and pull me back. We do life together despite, in some cases, living many hours from each other. We make each other a priority.

I'm so grateful for these brothers, and so proud of them and their wives. They have wisdom and stature…and humility. They live lives of joy and have journeyed well, raising great kids. Their roots run deep, and they bear fruit in season and out. To me, they are those trees thriving down by Four Mile Creek. And they help me thrive, a thought that is bringing tears to my eyes at this moment.

Mark Batterson writes: "Every generation must steward what's been entrusted to them. It starts with honoring the generation that has gone before us by learning everything we can from them…It continues by empowering the generation that comes after us."[2] I would also add, "It is sustained by walking with others who will be present with us in our current challenges."

Whom have you learned from? Who is in your personal Hall of Fame? Have you thanked them for their impact on you? Have you identified the difference their investment in you has made? What are you passing along from each Hall of Fame member to the next generation and the next?

Ideally, great go-to people should be:

- reliable,
- accessible,
- trustworthy,
- truth-telling,
- wise,
- productive,
- positive role models,
- challenging and encouraging,
- determined,
- successful in several areas of life;

and they should have:

- a good heart,
- strong values,
- true integrity,
- strength of character,
- a priority of service to others.

In other words, they're impact players who are successful in multiple areas of life rather than specializing in only one area. The best people to journey with have the power and ability to affect others based on who they are, not just on what they do. They paint whatever they're representing with such quality that people notice and are inspired to greatness themselves.

One Major League Baseball team president said of the manager he hired: "His personality and his intellect and his heart are almost too big not to make a difference in whatever organization he's in.

He creates possibility. He's one of a certain subset today that creates opportunities for an organization just by his mere presence."[3]

These are the kinds of people you want to bring with you. They will help you get where you intend to go. They encourage you to be your BEST. Just don't forget to repay the favor. Make sure you're a go-to person for others. Be a leader who serves, not a self-serving leader. That's the essence of leading yourself.

Are you ready? Grab your gear and your team, and let's go! Your dreams and destiny are waiting.

THE DESTINY BEYOND YOUR DESTINATION

They often called him "Forty-One," although there was a time in his life when he was number one on the world's stage.

The son of a US senator and a loving, humble mother, he enlisted in the Navy on his eighteenth birthday, just months after the Japanese attack on Pearl Harbor. His parents had hoped he'd go to college first and then join the military. That's what his classmates were being encouraged to do...and it's what nearly all of them did. But feeling compelled to serve his country, he took a different path, earning his wings while still eighteen years old and becoming the second-youngest fighter pilot in World War II.

He was awarded four times for his heroism, including the Distinguished Flying Cross. After fifty-eight combat missions, he returned home to the States, married his high school sweetheart, graduated from Yale, enjoyed great business success, and then felt the call to government service. There were some electoral defeats and personal setbacks on his life's journey, but he kept pressing on, and the esteem of his titles grew, from congressman to ambassador, to CIA director, and then vice president. His ultimate rise to the position of "leader of the Western world," however, marked the height of his success in history's eyes.

Being number one is a huge accomplishment. Yet, as so many who knew him have attested, he cared more about the significance of numbers such as seventy-three, six, seventeen, and forty-three. They denote a life by design, spent in the pursuit of service to his family, his constituents, and his country.

Seventy-three was the number of years he was married to his wife before she died in April 2018. In an anniversary letter to her, he wrote: "I've climbed perhaps the highest mountain in the world [that of being president of the United States], but even that cannot hold a candle to being Barbara's husband."[1]

The couple had six children and seventeen grandchildren. The entire family has dedicated their lives to the service of others—some of them privately, leading businesses and global philanthropic efforts, mentoring programs, and childhood literacy and volunteer initiatives, and some of them in the most public political offices. Their eldest was nicknamed "Forty-Three," because he followed in his father's footsteps, all the way to the White House; another son became a two-time governor of the state of Florida.

When his journey on this earth was done, they remembered George Herbert Walker Bush most for the man he was, not the positions he held or the political dynasty he and wife Barbara raised.

Wrote Lauren Hubbard after Bush's passing on November 30, 2018, "Perhaps his most lasting legacy will remain that of a family man."[2]

He was remembered as "the best father a son or daughter could have" (stated George W. in his eulogy). For making each of his family members feel "adored" (remarked his granddaughter Jenna in her *TODAY* show tribute).[3] For being "the greatest human being that I will ever know" (tweeted son Jeb). For encouraging his family to "do what you can to help the world" (recalled his grandson George P. Bush).

H.W. himself said, "Be bold in your dreaming, be bold in your living, be bold in your caring, your compassion, your humility."[4] These were principles he lived by in his interactions with family, foes, and friends alike. Kaylee Hartung of CNN wrote: "Whether you're a fan of his policies and presidential record or not, those who have met him tend to agree that he treated people with kindness."[5] She reports that, upon leaving the Oval Office after being soundly defeated by Democrat Bill Clinton in the 1992 presidential race, Republican George H. W. Bush left his successor a letter that included these gracious words: "Your success now is our country's success. I am rooting hard for you."

And though the elder Bush was deeply disappointed at not being reelected, he and Clinton became close friends in their post-presidential years. "No relationship is quite like the bond between George H. W. Bush and the man who defeated him in 1992," wrote Nancy Gibbs and Michael Duffy in their book *The Presidents Club*. "Bush would go so far as to suggest more than once that he might be the father that Clinton had always lacked—a notion that the younger man did not dispute."[6]

There were others to whom the elder Bush became a mentor or

father figure. The list includes Jim Nantz and Arnold Schwarzenegger. But Clinton and Bush were indeed a surprise pairing. Once they looked past their political differences, they found commonality in their global concerns and joined forces more than once to raise millions of dollars to help others, first in the wake of the 2004 Indian Ocean tsunami, and again after Hurricane Katrina rocked New Orleans.

Bush continued to privately serve and support others in numerous ways until his death. Private citizens and public figures (not to mention his friends and family) spoke of his handwritten letters and notes—a legacy of words to a world of people, including folks he never met and opponents who had once sided against him. Thousands of those letters exist. It was one of the many ways he gave of himself.

"He never stopped serving...," Clinton said. "His remarkable leadership and great heart were always on full display. I...will always hold our friendship as one of my life's greatest gifts."[7]

He never stopped adventuring, either. In his eulogy of his father, George W. Bush remarked how his dad maintained a spirit of adventure even in his later years. He'd open the engines on his speedboat and "joyfully fly across the Atlantic with the Secret Service boats straining to keep up." On his seventy-fifth, eightieth, eighty-fifth, and ninetieth birthdays, H.W. parachuted out of a plane.

His life consisted of one uncommon adventure after another, just as any of ours can. But his greatest was the adventure of the heart: "[Dad] recognized that serving others enriched the giver's soul," said W. "Well, Dad, we're going to remember you for exactly that and so much more. And we're going to miss you. Your decency, sincerity, and kind soul will stay with us forever."

WHAT WE HOPE TO LEAVE BEHIND

I reflected on so many of these things as Cindy and I stood outside the Capitol Building in December 2018, where thousands were paying their respects to the Bush family as the former president's body lay in state. Whereas many people live their lives looking out for number one, Bush's life represented a far greater force: the multiplied power of one.

One person.

Leading himself by design.

For a lifetime.

For the sake of others.

That is the destiny each of us is meant for, the destiny beyond all the destinations we may see in our lifetimes.

Yes, leading yourself often paves the way to heightened success. Yes, it qualifies you to lead others. But more importantly, it positions you to live *for* others—to raise up more leaders who serve, not more followers who only serve themselves. Someone has said that "great leaders don't set out to be a leader. They set out to make a difference. It's never about the role, it's always about the goal"—goals such as an impact greater than income. Presence over platform. Character, not just conduct.

Are you making a difference, or just a living? It all depends on who you're living for. Business guru Jack Welch, the former CEO of General Electric, wrote in his book *Winning*: "Before you are a leader, success is all about growing yourself. When you become a leader, success is all about growing others."[8] More than anything else, this book is about the fact that there is a destiny beyond your destinations. It's the legacy you create—what you bequeath to others while you live that will serve them after you die; what people inherit of your character, your wisdom, your values, your ways that helps them on their way—along with the love you give.

Bush recognized this, and said so in his inaugural address: "We cannot hope only to leave our children a bigger car, a bigger bank account. We must hope to give them a sense of what it means to be a loyal friend, a loving parent, a citizen who leaves his home, his neighborhood and town better than he found it. What do we want the men and women who work with us to say when we are no longer there? That we were more driven to succeed than anyone around us, or that we stopped to ask if a sick child had gotten better and stayed a moment there to trade a word of friendship?"

And here's the difference it made: Tellingly, his final words on this side of heaven were not about him or his feats. They were, "I love you, too," spoken to one of his children—the hallmark of a life of significance, lived from the heart.

HOW DREAMS LIVE ON

In his book *Chase the Lion*, Mark Batterson sums up the destiny beyond our destinations in this way: "Your legacy isn't your dream. Your legacy is leveraging the dreams of those who come after you… Simply put, success is succession. That's how our dreams outlive us. They live on in the second-generation dreams that we inspire."[9]

I love Batterson's play on words—that "success is succession." The pursuit of significance is what inspires the dreams and betters the lives of people you'll never meet, three and four and seven generations after you, not just the one or two generations that know you personally.

Abraham Lincoln knew that were his efforts to abolish slavery in America successful, it would set a new course not only for "the millions now in bondage [to slavery], but of unborn millions to come."[10] Lincoln had his eyes on those distant generations, says Batterson. His dream wasn't about him. It was about the lives of those whose world he would never live to see.

Maybe your own life won't alter world history, as Lincoln's and Bush's did. But what if, simply because you choose to live by design, you influence that one person—your son or daughter, a neighborhood kid, that new hire at work—who goes on to change the trajectory of life for millions of people? None of us can say this isn't possible. You don't have to be a statesman or a celebrity—and neither do the people you touch. But someone in your circle might well have just that kind of impact, all because you chose to lead yourself to a life of significance.

You have complete say over where you're headed and who you're living for. Hopefully, through this book, you've decided to live for others and not just yourself—and you've identified who those others are. With those decisions made, keep pushing for significance. Live to serve. Write so well on the slate of those people's hearts that they are forever changed for having known you. And whatever you've been given to do as your purpose, finish it.

MARKED BY JOY

There's more to my Longs Peak experience than I have told you. I was fifty-five years old and had decided that reaching the top was too hard for me. I'd done triathlons and marathons in my younger days, but this was harder, particularly at my age. Still, Cindy and my sons knew that summiting was on my Lifetime List, and so they persuaded me to give it another try—with them.

The fact that I had written off Longs Peak as a possibility ("I'm too old"; "It's too hard") was symptomatic of a bigger issue in my life. Other pursuits were falling into that same category. I had become more passive, less proactive. Our financial-services firm had come through a time when things had gone poorly, and it was my fault. I had lost some confidence in my business life and, more broadly, in my personal life. I was spiritually flat and distant. My energy and enthusiasm were well below par. I was stuck.

When Cindy called me to tell me that our friend John Ramsey was going to climb Longs Peak, she was sure that I should go with him. But I was still reluctant, hindered by strong doubt and anxiety. In order to avoid the issue, I said I would do it only if one or two of the Reeter boys could do it with me. I was thinking, or I guess hoping, that they wouldn't be able to participate this time around. I knew Chad couldn't because he had very limited time off from work. Remarkably, though, Cindy called me back very shortly and said, "Both Ryan and Cody want to do it with you." I had two immediate and contrasting reactions: *Ugh* and *Game on!*

Unlike the first time, when Cindy and I had tried the climb, there would be no chance to train. I was in decent shape from my normal exercise regimen, but not in climbing shape. The boys and I arrived in Colorado a little early to acclimate to the altitude and do some easy climbs. The afternoon before the climb, we drove over to Estes Park, bought some trail food at the grocery store, "carbed up" with a pasta meal, and went to bed. None of us slept a wink.

We departed at one thirty in the morning with headlamps. John Ramsey, an experienced climber as well as a several-time conqueror of Longs Peak, would be our leader for the fifteen-mile adventure. John and his wife, Jerri, had summited the same day that Cindy and I had discontinued our climb fifteen years earlier. Our group would be attempting the seven and a half miles up and the seven and a half miles back, all in one day.

Not far into our ascent, Cody threw up. "Dude, you okay?" I asked. "Oh yeah, it's nothin'," he said. Over the next five miles, he threw up several more times, continually assuring us, "No big deal. Let's just keep hiking." Despite the nausea, he was unwilling to stop or turn back. But before we reached the Boulder Field, it was John (who was also a physician) who declared that Cody could no longer continue. His loss of sustenance was not only putting him in danger but would prevent him from being physically able to reach the summit.

I told Cody, "I'll hike down with you." He was emphatic: "No way, Dad! You go on and reach the summit. I'll be fine hiking down." Knowing I wasn't going to persuade him otherwise, I continued on with the rest of our crew.

The last couple of miles were difficult and dangerous. The words of a close friend who worked at a camp nearby came to mind more than once. He had pulled me aside the afternoon before and urged me not to pursue the summit. "Every year, people fall to their death on those Ledges," he'd said.

We traversed the Boulder Field, got through the Keyhole, across the Ledges, and navigated the Narrows. The final push was really, really tough for me. The altitude there is so high that it's hard to catch your breath. Ryan was doing well, but he became worried about me, asking a couple of times if I was okay. I tried to say, "Sure," rather nonchalantly, but I think he knew I was struggling.

Finally, as we scaled the last granite wall, the two of us were near each other. Ryan, though, beat me to the top. As I crested the summit, he reached out his hand, pulled me up into a big hug, and said, "I'm proud of you, Dad!" What a fantastic, unforgettable moment! What a remarkable role reversal for my grown son to be proud of me.

Our family loves pictures, so we took a few right there. Those mountaintop photos are extremely meaningful to me—certainly, for the sake of a lifetime goal accomplished, but what mattered most, and still does to this day, was that full-circle, multigenerational experience with Ryan and Cody. It had been a lifetime in the making, and the exuberance I felt at having taken this uncommon adventure with them is something I draw from often. It helps fuel my other pursuits.

Though heading down the mountain was no piece of cake, either, we again found a way. As we departed the treacherous areas and took the descending trail to the foot of Longs Peak, I had on my headphones, and tears were just streaming down my face because my heart was so full. That day's playlist had been preloaded by my team specifically for that climb. I listened to Steven Curtis Chapman's "The Great Adventure" on the way down, and Miley Cyrus's "The Climb," which was especially touching. It talked about having your faith shaken but climbing on anyway, stating that there's always going to be another mountain, so we don't dare quit. Rachel Platten's "Fight Song" was also on the list, along with the John Denver throwback "Rocky Mountain High."

I couldn't have asked for more. In a matter of twenty-four hours, I'd traveled from being stuck in fear and survival mode, to the successful completion of a lifelong goal, to a legacy moment where I'd witnessed the maturity of my own sons. Its significance was striking, and the joy I felt has never gone away.

THE UNCOMMON LIFE

A life of adventure is one thing. Bush lived it in spades, and my family and I are trying to also. But leading oneself to a life of uncommon adventures, with significance always in your sights, is the greater journey. You're not only engaging wholeheartedly in your own passionate pursuit, but you're offering up your very best to the others who are traveling beside you and behind you. It's not common, but it is "the high life." And nothing can keep you from this highest of callings if you'll claim it as your destiny.

Whatever adventures you're taking on, whatever your goals or mountains you've decided to climb, MAP them out and go after them. And as you do, bring along as many people as you can. Whatever you've set your mind and heart to do—especially those pursuits for the good of others—do them with all your might. We have a great cloud of witnesses surrounding and/or watching us, so let's pay attention to that age-old statement to throw off everything that entangles us or encumbers us and run, hike, climb, pursue with positive energy and perseverance this journey, this race, the adventure of life set before us with our eyes fixed on truth and faith!

You and those you love will never be the same.

ACKNOWLEDGMENTS

As a brand new author, I have tremendous gratitude for the team around me who have spent countless hours shoring up my many deficiencies!

To Kris Bearss, my fantastic teammate in pulling this crazy, multidimensional manuscript together: I'm so grateful to you for your wonderful capacity, creativity, and detail to follow-through. I'm struck by your ability to completely comprehend my heart for this important message. Thanks for being the glue that holds this whole project together. Thank you, from the bottom of my heart, for your countless hours of hard work and exemplary leadership!

To Sealy Yates (Yates & Yates), my renowned literary agent: Thank you for your steadfast friendship and tremendous care for this project. I have come to realize that the message in this book is very much the message and story of your iconic life pursuit. You are a tremendous role model of doing life differently. You are an impeccable person who chooses life by design, not by default.

To Cindy Reeter, to whom this book is dedicated (along with our sons): Thanks for being a critical editor and sage, wise counsel in the creation of this manuscript. Given our journey together of thirty-three-plus years, it's no surprise that you have held me in check!

To our team at the Texas Financial Group: You guys are such a great inspiration for getting this message out. Thanks for doing life with me.

NOTES

CHAPTER 1: LOST AND FOUND

1 "Shaping Future Leaders: Tools for Creating a Culture of Leadership Development," Facts and Trends, LifeWay, updated September 28, 2015, https://factsandtrends.net/2015/09/28/shaping-future-leaders/.

2 Jim Collins, *Good to Great: Why Some Companies Make the Leap…and Others Don't* (New York: HarperCollins, 2001), 1.

CHAPTER 2: DEFAULT OR DESIGN? YOUR CRITICAL CHOICE

1 Peter Drucker, during a classroom lecture, in William A. Cohen, *Drucker on Leadership: New Lessons from the Father of Modern Management* (New York: John Wiley and Sons, 2010), 4.

2 Rob Asghar (paraphrasing Warren Bennis), "Why Real Leaders Don't Set Out to Become Leaders," Forbes, updated June 16, 2014, https://www.forbes.com/sites/robasghar/2014/06/16/why-real-leaders-dont-set-out-to-become-leaders/#2da8cf2f1e08/.

3 Oprah Winfrey, *What I Know for Sure*, read by the author (New York: Macmillan Audio, 2014).

4 Asghar, "Why Real Leaders Don't Set Out to Become Leaders."

5 Warren Bennis, *An Invented Life: Reflections on Leadership and Change* (New York: Basic Books, 1994).

CHAPTER 3: THE SIGNIFICANCE OF SIGNIFICANCE

1 Alan Arnette, "Everest FAQ," AlanArnette.com, accessed August 1, 2019, http://www.alanarnette.com/everest/everestfaq.php/.

2 Alan Arnette, "Everest Base Camp 2016," May 3, 2016, YouTube video, https://www.youtube.com/watch?v=GybCbOYizzI/. See also AlanArnette.com.

3 Pablo S. Torre, "How (and Why) Athletes Go Broke," Vault, *Sports Illustrated*, updated March 23, 2009, https://www.si.com /vault/2009/03/23/105789480/how-and-why-athletes-go-broke/.

CHAPTER 4: YOUR PEAK EXISTENCE

1 Psalm 1:3 (New International Version).

2 Robert Crosby, *The One Jesus Loves: Grace Is Unconditionally Given, Intimacy Must Be Relentlessly Pursued* (Nashville: Thomas Nelson, 2014).

CHAPTER 5: YOUR JOURNEY TILL NOW

1 John F. Kennedy, "Address at Rice University on the Nation's Space Effort," John F. Kennedy Presidential Library and Museum, September 12, 1962, https://www.jfklibrary.org/learn/about-jfk/historic-speeches /address-at-rice-university-on-the-nations-space-effort.

2 Ben Carson, *You Have a Brain: A Teen's Guide to T.H.I.N.K. B.I.G.* (Grand Rapids: Zondervan, 2015), 17.

3 See Carson, *You Have a Brain*, 54–57.

4 Charles Swindoll, *Improving Your Serve* in *The Inspirational Writings of Charles Swindoll: Improving Your Serve, Strengthening Your Grip, Dropping Your Guard—Three Bestselling Works in One Volume* (New York: Inspirational Press, 1994), 301.

5 Jamais Cascio, "The Next Big Thing: Resilience," *FP* (September 28, 2009), https://foreignpolicy.com/2009/09/28/the-next-big-thing -resilience/.

6 Swindoll, *Improving Your Serve* in *The Inspirational Writings,* 301.

CHAPTER 6: WHERE AM I GOING?

1 Stephen R. Covey, *The 7 Habits of Highly Effective People: Powerful Lessons in Personal Change* (New York: Free Press, 2004), 95.

2   Mark Batterson, *Chase the Lion: If Your Dream Doesn't Scare You, It's Too Small* (Colorado Springs: Multnomah, 2018).

3   Santokh Singh, "Critical Reasons for Crashes Investigated in the National Motor Vehicle Crash Causation Survey," Crash Stats, Traffic Safety Facts, US Department of Transportation, https://crashstats .nhtsa.dot.gov/Api/Public/ViewPublication/812115/.

4   Guy Finley, "Everything You Need to Know About the Dark Night of the Soul," Wisdom School Special Lesson, guyfinley.org (posted January 17, 2020), https://www.guyfinley.org/everything-you-need-to -know-about-the-dark-night-of-the-soul-29540.html.

5   *A Football Life*, "Mike Singletary," aired November 13, 2015, on NFL Network.

CHAPTER 7: STUCK

1   Lynne Twist, *The Soul of Money: Reclaiming the Wealth of Our Inner Resources* (New York: W. W. Norton, 2017), 120.

2   Twist, *Soul of Money*, 121.

CHAPTER 8: GETTING UNSTUCK

1   Shawn Brown, "Mike Singletary: 'Christ Means Everything,'" *The 700 Club*, http://www1.cbn.com/mike-singletary-christ-means-everything.

2   Charley Shimanski, "General Back Country Safety: A Resource for All Back Country Users," Mountain Rescue Assocation, updated 2008, https://mra.org/wp-content/uploads/2016/05/backcountrysafety.pdf, 12.

3   Twist, *The Soul of Money*, 121–22.

4   Collins refers to this idea as "The Stockdale Paradox." See Collins, *Good to Great*, 83–85.

5   Collins, *Good to Great*, 13 (emphasis mine).

6   Collins, *Good to Great*, 85.

7   See Maureen Callahan, "Tortured in Notorious 'Hanoi Hilton,' 11 GIs Were Unbreakable," *New York Post*, updated February 15, 2014, http:// nypost.com/2014/02/15/tortured-in-vietnams-worst-prison-11

-us-soldiers-were-unbreakable/. See Alvin Townley, *Defiant: The POWs Who Endured Vietnam's Most Infamous Prison, the Women Who Fought for Them, and the One Who Never Returned* (New York: Thomas Dunne Books, 2014).

CHAPTER 9: THE PASSIONATE PURSUIT

1 1 John 4:18 (English Standard Version).

2 Helen Keller in letter to Rev. Phillips Brooks, South Boston, June 8, 1881. See Helen Keller Archive at the American Foundation for the Blind, https://www.afb.org/HelenKellerArchive?a=d&d=A-HK02 -B229-F01-012.1.1&srpos=1&e=-------en-20--1--txt--%22best+and +most+beautiful+things+in+the+world%22------3-7-6-5-3 --------------0-1.

3 The actual quote was: "There can be no definition of a successful life that does not include service to others." George H. W. Bush, *All the Best, George Bush: My Life in Letters and Other Writings* (New York: Scribner, 2014), 646.

4 My paraphrase of Jesus's words in Mark 9:35.

CHAPTER 10: LIFE ON PURPOSE

1 Annie F. Downs, "Let me back up and tell you how we got here...," Instagram photo, July 25, 2018, https://www.instagram.com/p /BlprhnsFaVr/?taken-by=anniefdowns.

2 Exodus 33:13 (King James Version).

3 See Exodus 33:14–15.

CHAPTER 11: THE HABITS OF SIGNIFICANCE

1 Will Durant, *The Story of Philosophy: The Lives and Opinions of the World's Greatest Philosophers* (New York: Simon and Schuster, 1926), 87.

2 Psalm 16:7 (New Living Translation).

CHAPTER 12: WHAT (AND WHO) WE TAKE WITH US

1 https://www.thenorthface.com/about-us/outdoor-exploration/about -the-explore-fund.html.

2 Batterson, *Chase the Lion*, 191.

3 Tom Verducci (quoting Theo Epstein on Joe Maddon), *The Cubs Way: The Zen of Building the Best Team in Baseball and Breaking the Curse* (New York: Crown Archetype, 2017), 187.

EPILOGUE: THE DESTINY BEYOND YOUR DESTINATION

1 Forty-ninth anniversary letter dated January 6, 1994, shared in Barbara Bush, *Pearls of Wisdom: Little Pieces of Advice (That Go a Long Way)* (New York: Twelve), 43.

2 Lauren Hubbard, "How George H. W. Bush's Extraordinary Political Career Shaped His Relationship with His Children," *Town and Country*, updated December 5, 2018, https://www .townandcountrymag.com/society/politics/a25367255/george-hw -bush-barbara-bush-children/.

3 "Jenna Bush Hager Shares Love Letter to Her 'Gampy,' George H. W. Bush," TODAY.com (December 3, 2018), https://www.today.com /news/jenna-bush-hager-shares-love-letter-her-gampy-george-h -t144281.

4 The whole quote is from his Johns Hopkins University commencement speech (May 22, 1996), https://hub.jhu.edu/2018/12/05/george-hw -bush-commencement/

5 Kaylee Hartung, "George H. W. Bush was a prolific letter-writer. Here's how one of his letters touched my family," cnn.com (December 4, 2018), https://www.cnn.com/2018/12/04/politics/kaylee-hartung -reporters-notebook-bush/index.html.

6 Nancy Gibbs and Michael Duffy, *The Presidents Club: Inside the World's Most Exclusive Fraternity* (New York: Simon and Schuster, 2013). In Ashley Fetters, "How George H. W. Bush and Bill Clinton Went from

Political Rivals to Best Friends," *Atlantic*, updated December 2, 2018, https://www.theatlantic.com/politics/archive/2018/12/george -h-w-bush-and-bill-clintons-famous-friendship/577147/.

7   David Mark (quoting Bill Clinton), "George H. W. Bush and Bill Clinton: From Fierce Rivals to Close Friends," *Washington Examiner*, updated December 1, 2018, https://www.washingtonexaminer.com /news/george-h-w-bush-and-bill-clinton-from-fierce-rivals-to-close -friends.

8   Jack Welch with Suzy Welch, *Winning: The Ultimate Business How-to Book*, Kindle edition (New York: HarperBusiness, 2009).

9   Batterson, *Chase the Lion*, 162.

10 New-York Historical Society Museum and Library, "The Thirteenth Amendment" (February 1–April 30, 2012), Exhibitions page, https:// www.nyhistory.org/exhibitions/the-thirteenth-amendment.

ABOUT THE AUTHOR

Author and speaker **JEFF D. REETER** pursues life by design as an entrepreneur, servant leader, and strategist. His mission in organizational leadership is wholly developing teams of champions dedicated to excellence in serving others. He is often heard up and down the halls of his financial firm (Northwestern Mutual) saying, "Seek first to serve, love, care, matter, make a difference, and be a catalyst in the life of another person and see if everything else doesn't work out for you."

Jeff is married to Cindy and enjoys outdoor adventures (hiking, fishing, hunting, etc.) and spending time at the Reeter Ranch with their family and friends.